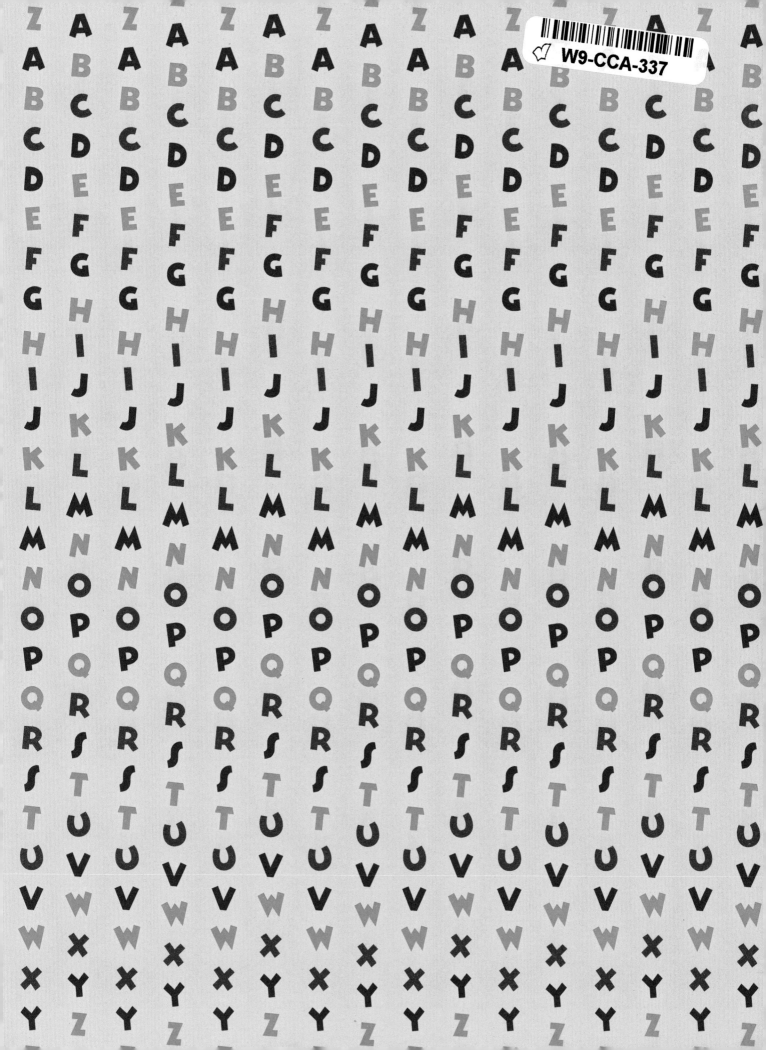

MY FIRST DICTIONARY

Susan Miller, Ed.D.

Publications International, Ltd.

Susan Miller, Ed.D., is professor emeritus of early childhood education at Kutztown University of Pennsylvania. She has written for more than 250 journals, magazines, and books, including *Scholastic's Early Childhood Today, Childhood Education, Early Childhood News,* and the weekend activities for *Parent & Child* magazine. Miller is a frequent presenter at conferences for the National Association for the Education of Young Children and the Association of Childhood Education International Study.

Illustrations by Ted Williams

Photography by Brian Warling Photography and Siede Preis Photography

Louis Weber, CEO
Publications International, Ltd.
7373 North Cicero Avenue
Lincolnwood, Illinois 60712

www.myactiveminds.com

Permission is never granted for commercial purposes.

ActiveMinds® is a registered trademark of Publications international, Ltd.

ISBN-13: 978-0-7853-8369-7
ISBN-10: 0-7853-8369-7

Manufactured in China.

8 7 6 5 4 3 2 1

Library of Congress Control Number: 2003103997

HOW TO USE THIS DICTIONARY

Why This Dictionary Is Helpful for Children

My First Dictionary is written for young children showing an interest in how to use words and letters. It is also for children beginning to learn to read who want to sharpen their writing and spelling skills.

At first, children may want to use the illustrations or photos on each page to match the meanings to the words. As their reading skills emerge, they will enjoy using the dictionary to spell words and look up their meanings. *My First Dictionary* is designed for young children to use alone or with the assistance of an adult.

What Is a Dictionary?

A dictionary is a very special type of book. It doesn't tell a story like most of the books children may be used to reading. Instead, it is filled with all kinds of information about words that will help children to read, write, or tell stories of their own.

The words in this dictionary come from many places. Some words are used every day, while others may be seen or heard on television. There are words about groups of things that interest children

(such as animals or toys) and words from vocabulary lists that teachers think children should know.

The words in a dictionary are arranged differently than in other books. The words are arranged in lists that go down the page, rather than across the page in sentences and paragraphs. A dictionary is easy to use when you understand how it is designed. Let's take a look at the setup for *My First Dictionary.*

How to Find Words

Because there are so many words in a dictionary, young readers could easily become confused if they tried to find a certain word. Fortunately, all of the words are arranged in alphabetical order. What this means is that just like the alphabet, all of the words that begin with the letter *A* come first, and then those that start with the letter *B* are next. The words that begin with *Z* come at the very end of the dictionary.

On the top of each page in this dictionary, there will be one of two things. It may be a large letter, such as a *D*. This means that the list of all the words starting with *D* begins on that page. Or it may be two *guide words,*

such as *ask–ax.* This shows the first and last words on that page, and it also shows where the words are in the alphabet. These words will help readers narrow their focus when looking for a specific word.

Readers may also notice all of the letters of the alphabet in order on the side of each page. This is to help if children need to know which letters come before or after each other in alphabetical order when they are looking up words in the dictionary. There will be a big arrow next to the starting letter of words featured on that page.

Children can search for particular words that they want to know more about. They will see lists of words printed in bold. These words are called *entry words.* They show readers the correct way to spell words when they want to write them.

Children should be sure to use the alphabet to help find the entry word they are looking for on a page. First, they can think of the letter the word begins with. For instance, *leaf* starts with an *l.* Readers can search for the *L* section and then look at the next letter in the

word. They will find the words that start with *le* and then look at the *le* words until they find *leaf.* Sometimes, they might have to go to the third letter in the word, for example *lea,* for help.

Using Definitions

The meaning of a word, or the *definition,* tells something about it. There are usually one or two sentences that give this information. Some words have more than one meaning and can be used in different ways. The various meanings a word has are given separately and have numbers in front of them.

Often, readers will see a sentence written in *italics* after the definition. That lets them see how they can use the word. Frequently, a picture or photo will give another clue about how the word is used.

The Way Words Are Used

Sometimes words can have different spellings depending on how they are used. For instance, *rests* and *resting* are forms of the word *rest,* but they are spelled differently because they have slightly different uses. Words that describe more than one thing are called plural. Most words simply add an *s* to become plural *(doll, dolls),* but others change in special ways. The word *mouse,* for

example, changes to *mice* when there is more than one mouse. Other words add an *es (church, churches).* In a few words, the final *y* changes to *i,* and an *es* is added *(story, stories).* In *My First Dictionary,* you can see how a word becomes plural. Right below the entry word, you will sometimes see plurals in parentheses ( ). Words that add *s* to become plural will not appear in parentheses, but words that become plural in any other way will feature their plural form in the parentheses.

Other words describe action. They can also change their spelling depending on how they are used. When someone is speaking about something that happened in the past or the present, the spelling will sometimes

change. Examples of this are *look, looks, looked, looking* and *go, goes, went, gone, going.* In *My First Dictionary,* every action word will be followed by parentheses that include how the word is used for something that happens now, for something that

happened in the past, and for something that is in the middle of happening now. As an example, the word *say* will be followed by *(says, said, saying).*

Some words that compare things change their spelling, as well. Many times these words add *er* for more and *est* for the most (such as *fast, faster, fastest*). Other words change their spelling completely (such as *good, better, best*). Words in parentheses will demonstrate how these words are spelled when they refer to more and most.

Finally, readers will notice that most words begin with lowercase letters. However, some words begin with uppercase, capital letters. Words for holidays, such as *Thanksgiving,* days, such as *Monday,* and months, such as *November,* start with capital letters.

All Set to Begin

My First Dictionary will be an exciting tool to help children use and find out more about words as they read, write, spell, and listen to others. Remember that children learn best with the help of adults such as parents and teachers, so children should always be ready to ask for help if they need it.

a
A means one of something. *They rode to school on **a** bus.*

about
1. **About** means almost. *Four cookies are **about** a handful.* 2. Sometimes **about** means nearby. *The children are playing **about**.*

above
Above means higher than something. *The pear is **above** the lemon.*

acorn
An **acorn** is a kind of nut that grows on an oak tree. Squirrels like to eat **acorns.**

across
If you go **across** something, you go from one side to the other. *The boy walked **across** the road.*

act
(acts, acted, acting)
When people take part in a play, they **act** in it. *The boys were **acting** like knights in the play.*

action
Taking **action** is doing something. *Running is a very fast **action**.*

add
(adds, added, adding)
If you **add** things, you put them together. *You **add** one block on top of another to build a tower.*

address
(addresses)
An **address** tells people where you live. *You write an **address** on a letter before you mail it.*

adult
An **adult** is a grown-up person such as your teacher.

afraid

If you are **afraid,** you think something is bad or scary.

after

After means at a later time. *Most people eat breakfast **after** they wake up in the morning.*

afternoon

The **afternoon** is the part of the day that happens after the morning.

again

Again means something occurs once more. *The child asked to sing the favorite song **again.***

against

1. When something is **against** another thing, it is touching it. *The pear leans **against** the lemon.* 2. **Against** can also mean on the other side. *When you play a game, you are **against** the other players.*

age

Your **age** tells how old you are. Your **age** is the number of years you have been alive.

ago

Ago means earlier than now. *You were a baby a long time **ago.***

ahead

When you are **ahead,** you are in front of something. *You win the race when you finish **ahead** of the other runners.*

air

Air is a gas we breathe. The **air** is all around us.

airplane

An **airplane** is a machine that flies through the air. People can sit inside an **airplane** when they fly. An **airplane** has wings and an engine.

alarm

An **alarm** is a sound that gets your attention for a reason. *When the **alarm** in a clock rings, it tells you it is time to wake up.*

album

An **album** is a book that holds pictures. *You can put pictures of your family in a photo **album.***

alike

If two things are **alike,** they are the same in some way. *An orange and an apple are **alike** because they are both fruit.*

all

All means every one. ***All** of the cookies are round.*

alligator

An **alligator** is a scaly animal with a long mouth, sharp teeth, and a long tail. An **alligator** can swim in water or walk on land.

almond

An **almond** is a kind of nut with a light brown shell. Some candy bars contain **almonds.**

almost

Almost means nearly or not quite. *You are **almost** tall enough to reach the window.*

alone

When you are **alone,** you are not with other people.

along

Along means at a point beside a line. *You have buttons **along** the front of your coat.*

alphabet

The **alphabet** has all the letters that make words. There are 26 letters from *A* to *Z* in the **alphabet.**

already

Already means before or by this time. *You can have dessert if you **already** ate your lunch.*

also

Also means in addition to. *You may **also** get some pizza to go with your juice.*

always

Always means all of the time. *You always get wet when you take a bath.*

am

(be, are, is, was, were, been, being)
Am means that someone or something exists. *I am the best bike rider.*

among

Among means in between or in the middle of things. *The pear is among the lemons.*

an

An means one of something. *You are eating an apple.*

anchor

An **anchor** keeps something in place. *The heavy anchor sinks through the water to keep a ship from moving.*

and

And is used to connect two things. *You need a ball and a bat to play baseball.*

angry

(angrier, angriest)
If you are **angry,** you feel mad and upset. *An angry person may want to yell.*

animal

An **animal** lives, moves, and breathes. *People, dogs, birds, and fish are animals.*

another

Another means one more. *Would you like another glass of milk?*

answer

(answers, answered, answering)
1. When you **answer,** you talk to someone who asked you a question.
2. What you say or write down after a question is an **answer.**

ant

An **ant** is a tiny crawling insect. Most **ants** live in tunnels underground.

antenna

(antennae)
An **antenna** is part of a TV or radio. An **antenna** picks up signals that become sounds and pictures for you to hear and see.

any

1. **Any** means one is not more important than another. If you can chose **any,** it doesn't matter which one you choose. *You may pick **any** flower.*
2. **Any** also means an uncertain amount. *Is there **any** ice cream left?*

anyone

Anyone means one person is not more important than another. *You may pick **anyone** to play in your team.*

anything

1. **Anything** means one item is not more important than another. *You may play with **anything** in the toy box.*
2. **Anything** also means an uncertain thing. *Is there **anything** to do?*

ape

An **ape** is a hairy animal that can stand up straight. An **ape** is like a big monkey without a tail.

apple

An **apple** is a fruit that grows on trees. An **apple** is juicy and crunchy with red, green, or yellow skin.

apricot

An **apricot** is a sweet, juicy fruit that grows on trees. An **apricot** is yellow-orange with a big pit inside.

April

April is the fourth month of the year. **April** is in the springtime.

apron

An **apron** is a piece of clothing worn to keep your clothes clean.

are

(am, be, is, was, were, been, being)
Are means something occurs or lives. *You **are** going to school on the bus.*

arm

1. Your **arm** connects your shoulder and hand.
2. **Arms** are weapons, like guns or swords.

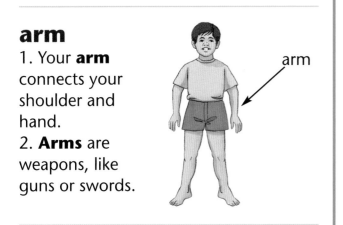

arm

army

(armies)
An **army** is a large group of people who fight together.

around

1. If you walk **around** the playground, you go along all the sides of it.
2. **Around** can also mean close to. *You might make a guess that it is **around** two o'clock.*

arrow

An arrow is a stick with a point on it. You use a bow to shoot an **arrow** at the target.

art

Something that someone has made, like a painting or drawing, is **art.**

artist

An **artist** is a person who draws, paints, or makes music.

as

As means like. *You are pretty **as** a picture.*

A B C D E F G H I J K L M N O P Q R S T U V W X Y Z

ask

(asks, asked, asking)
1. If you **ask** a question, you want an answer or help. 2. If you **ask** for something, you are saying you want it.

asparagus

Asparagus is a vegetable that grows in green or white spears.

astronaut

An **astronaut** is a person who goes into space. An **astronaut** wears a special suit and helmet.

at

At indicates a point in time or a place. *We will meet **at** one o'clock **at** the park.*

athlete

An **athlete** is a person who plays sports. **Athletes** can run, jump, and move around very well.

August

August is the eighth month of the year. **August** occurs in the summer.

aunt

Your **aunt** is the sister of your father or mother, or the wife of your uncle.

avocado

An **avocado** is a green or purple fruit that grows on trees. When ripe, an **avocado** is soft inside.

away

If you are **away,** you are missing from someplace because you are somewhere else. *We will go **away** on vacation.*

ax

(axes)
An **ax** is a tool with a long handle and sharp blade. You can chop wood with an **ax.** An **ax** is also a tool used by firefighters.

baby
(babies)
A **baby** is a very young child.

back
(backs, backed, backing)
1. If you **back** up your toy car, you move it behind the place where it was. 2. Your **back** is the part of your body below your neck. 3. The **back** is far away from the front of something. *The teacher wants you to move your desk to the **back** of the room.*

backpack
A **backpack** is a bag you wear on your back. You carry things like books and clothes in your **backpack.**

bad
(worse, worst)
1. If someone misbehaves, he is being naughty or **bad.** 2. If food is too old or not good to eat, it is **bad.**

badge
A person wears a **badge** to tell who she is. A **badge** may have the person's name or let you know about her job, like being a police officer.

bag
A **bag** is used to hold and carry things. **Bags** are made of paper, cloth, plastic, or leather.

bagel
A **bagel** is a chewy kind of bread shaped like a donut.

bake
(bakes, baked, baking)
You cook foods, such as bread or cookies, when you **bake** them in the oven. *We **baked** a birthday cake.*

baker
A **baker** is someone who cooks things in the oven. A **baker** sells the cakes and pies he baked.

ball

1. A **ball** is a round toy you roll, bounce, hit, throw, or catch.
2. A **ball** is a party where lots of people dance.

ballet

Ballet is a type of dancing where people spin and leap.

balloon

A **balloon** is a thin rubber or plastic bag that gets bigger when filled with air. Some balloons can float in the air.

banana

A **banana** is a long, curved fruit. A **banana** has yellow skin and a soft, white, tasty inside.

band

1. A **band** is a group of people who play music together. 2. A **band** is a thin piece of material that goes around something.

bandage

A **bandage** covers a cut or a sore to keep it clean.

banjo

A **banjo** is a musical instrument with strings you play with your fingers.

barn

A **barn** is a big building on a farm where the farmer keeps animals, hay, and machines.

barrette

A **barrette** is a clip to keep your hair in place.

baseball

1. A **baseball** is a hard ball the size of an apple.
2. **Baseball** is a game played by two teams with a ball and bat.

basket

A **basket** is used to hold or carry things. **Baskets** often have handles and are made of straw or sticks.

basketball

1. A **basketball** is a big ball that bounces. 2. In the game **basketball,** two teams try to throw the ball through a hoop.

bass

(bass)
A **bass** is a spiny-finned fish that swims in lakes and rivers.

bat

1. A **bat** is a stick used to hit a ball. 2. A **bat** is a small animal with wings that flies at night and sometimes lives in a cave.

bath

When you take a **bath,** you wash your body with water.

bathroom

A **bathroom** is a place with a sink and toilet and sometimes a tub or shower.

bathtub

A **bathtub** is something you fill up with water and then sit in to wash yourself.

battery

(batteries)
A **battery** gives something the energy it needs to work. A **battery** makes a toy work without plugging it in.

be

(am, are, is, was, were, been, being)
Be is used to show something occurs or something exists. *You can **be** a good baseball player if you practice.*

beach

(beaches)
A **beach** is a sandy place by the sea or a lake. You can swim and play at the **beach.**

bean

A **bean** is a kind of seed inside a vegetable. People eat many kinds of **beans**—kidney, lima, coffee, and green beans.

bear

A **bear** is a large furry animal. Many **bears** sleep all winter.

A B C D E F G H I J K L M N O P Q R S T U V W X Y Z

beard

A **beard** is the hair that grows on a man's chin and cheeks.

beat

(beats, beat, beaten, beating)
1. If you **beat** someone in a race, you win. 2. If you hit something over and over, you **beat** it. 3. The rhythm in music is the **beat.**

beautiful

If something is **beautiful,** it is lovely to see, to hear, or to smell.

beaver

A **beaver** is a furry animal with a flat tail and strong front teeth. **Beavers** build dams in streams.

because

Because tells the reason for something. *You are going to the store **because** you have run out of milk.*

become

(becomes, became, becoming)
If you **become** something, you turn into it. *If you eat your vegetables, you will **become** strong.*

bed

A **bed** is a soft place to lie down and rest or sleep.

bee

A **bee** is a small, flying, black-and-yellow insect that makes honey. If a **bee** gets angry, it might sting you.

beet

A **beet** is a garden vegetable. People eat the red root of a **beet.**

beetle

A **beetle** is a tiny insect with six legs. A **beetle** has hard wings.

before

1. **Before** means at an earlier time. *You got to school **before** I did.* 2. **Before** means in front of somebody or something. *The number one comes **before** two when you are counting.*

begin

(begins, began, begun, beginning)
If you **begin** something, you start it.

behind

If something is **behind** something else, it is at the back of it. *The pear is **behind** the lemon.*

---

believe

(believes, believed, believing)
If you **believe** somebody, you feel they are telling the truth.

---

bell

If you hit a **bell,** it makes a ringing sound. **Bells** are hollow and usually made of metal.

---

belong

(belongs, belonged, belonging)
If something **belongs** to you, it is yours.

---

below

If something is **below** another thing, it is under it. *The pear is **below** the lemon.*

---

belt

A **belt** is a long strip of cloth or leather that you wear around your waist. A **belt** holds up your pants.

bench

(benches)
A **bench** is a type of seat long enough for several people to sit on.

---

beneath

If something is under or lower than something else, it is **beneath** it.

---

berry

(berries)
A **berry** is a small, soft fruit with lots of seeds. There are many kinds of **berries,** such as blueberries, raspberries, and strawberries.

---

beside

Beside means that something is next to a thing or person. *The pear is **beside** the lemon.*

---

better

(good, best)
1. If you are feeling **better,** you are not as sick as you had been. 2. If you are good at something and practice hard, you will become **better** at it.

between

If something is **between** two things, it is in the middle of them. *The pear is between the lemons.*

beyond

If something is **beyond** reach, you are too far away from it to grab it.

bib

A **bib** is something a baby wears around his neck to keep food off his clothes.

bicycle

A **bicycle** is a machine you can ride. A **bicycle** has two wheels and a handlebar. You sit on the seat of the **bicycle** and pedal with your feet to make it go.

big

(bigger, biggest)
Big means something is not small.

binoculars

Binoculars are special glasses that make far-away things look like they are closer.

bird

A **bird** is an animal with a beak, wings, and feathers. Most **birds** can fly.

birth

A **birth** is the beginning of life when someone is born.

bite

(bites, bit, bitten, biting)
1. When you **bite** into something, you cut or grab it with your teeth. 2. A **bite** is a mouthful of food.

black

Black is the darkest color of all.

blanket

A **blanket** is a warm, thick cover for a bed.

block

(blocks, blocked, blocking)
1. If something **blocks** your way, you can't get through.
2. A **block** is a toy made out of wood or plastic that you can build with.

blood

Blood is a liquid that flows through veins inside your body.

blow

(blows, blew, blown, blowing)
When you **blow** air out of your mouth, or the wind **blows,** air moves.

blue

On a clear day, the sky is the color **blue.**

blueberry

(blueberries)

 A **blueberry** is a small, round, soft juicy fruit. **Blueberries** grow in bunches on a bush.

bluebird

A **bluebird** is a small, bluish songbird.

board

(boards, boarded, boarding)
1. You **board** a plane, train, or bus when you get on it to go on a trip. 2. A **board** is a long, flat piece of wood.

boat

A **boat** floats on the water and carries people or things. **Boats** move by engines, sails, or paddles.

body

(bodies)
Your **body** is all the parts of you put together. Some parts of an animal's or person's **body** are: head, back, eyes.

bone

A **bone** is the hard part inside your body under your skin. All of your **bones** together are called a skeleton.

bongo

A **bongo** is a small drum that you play with your hands.

bonnet

A **bonnet** is a cloth hat with ribbons that you tie under your chin.

book

A **book** is made up of a cover with sheets of paper inside called pages. You can look at pictures and read the words in a **book.**

boot

A **boot** is a tall shoe that covers your foot and part of your leg. **Boots** keep your feet warm and dry in cold, wet weather.

A B C D E F G H I J K L M N O P Q R S T U V W X Y Z

born

When a baby is **born,** its life begins outside of its mother.

boss

(bosses)

A **boss** is a leader or the person in charge of something.

both

Both means one and the other. *You and your sister are **both** playing with dolls.*

bottle

A **bottle** holds liquids. People can sometimes drink the liquid in a **bottle,** but sometimes they cannot. A baby's **bottle** has a special cap called a nipple.

bottom

The **bottom** of something, such as a lamp, is the base or the lowest part.

bounce

(bounces, bounced, bouncing)
When a ball **bounces,** it jumps back up again after it hits the ground.

bow

(bows, bowed, bowing)

1. When you **bow,** you bend over and lower your head. At the end of a show, performers **bow** to thank the audience for clapping. 2. A **bow** is a colorful ribbon that you tie. 3. A **bow** is used to shoot arrows. A stick is made into a **bow** when a string tied to both ends makes it curve.

bowl

(bowls, bowled, bowling)

1. When you **bowl,** you play a game to knock down pins with a bowling ball. 2. A **bowl** is a deep, round dish that holds food.

box

(boxes)

You can keep things in a wooden or cardboard **box** with four sides, a flat bottom, and a lid.

boy

A **boy** is a male child who grows up to be a man.

bracelet

A **bracelet** is a piece of pretty jewelry worn around the wrist.

branch
(branches)
A **branch** is the part of a tree with leaves that grows out from the trunk.

brave
(braver, bravest)
If people are **brave,** they do something they need to do, even if it frightens or might hurt them.

bread
Bread is a food made from flour and water and then baked in an oven. You can cut **bread** into slices to eat in a sandwich.

break
(breaks, broke, broken, breaking)
When you **break** something, it may not work any more. Sometimes things you **break** will divide into pieces.

breakfast
Breakfast is the first meal of the day. When you eat **breakfast,** you might have bread, fruit, and juice.

breathe
(breathes, breathed, breathing)
When you **breathe,** you bring air into your body through your nose and mouth and then send it out again.

brick
A **brick** is a block of baked clay. Many **bricks** stacked together make walls and buildings.

bridge
A **bridge** is something built over a road or water so that people can cross over from one side to the other.

briefcase
A **briefcase** is a box with a handle that people use to carry important papers to and from school or work.

bright
(brighter, brightest)
1. A **bright** color or light is strong and easy to see. 2. If someone is very smart, she is **bright.**

bring
(brings, brought, bringing)
If you **bring** something, you carry it with you.

broccoli

You eat the green stalk and buds of the green vegetable, **broccoli.**

broom

A **broom** is a long tool with straw on the wide end that you use to sweep the floor clean.

brother

Your **brother** is a boy who has the same mother or father as you.

brown

Brown is a dark color, like that of chocolate or toast.

bubble

A **bubble** is a thin skin of soap with a ball of air inside.

bug

A **bug** is any kind of small insect. A **bug** can move by flying, crawling, or jumping.

bugle

A **bugle** is a small brass horn without keys that makes a loud musical sound.

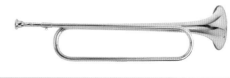

build

(builds, built, building)
If you **build** something, you put all of the parts together.

builder

A **builder** is a person who puts the parts together to make a building, such as a house, store, or shopping mall.

building

A **building** is a place that people create with walls and a roof. People live and work in **buildings** such as houses, schools, or barns.

bull

A **bull** is a male cow, a large farm animal with two long horns on its head. The **bull** eats grass and does not give milk.

bulldozer

A **bulldozer** is a big, heavy machine that has a blade on the front to push dirt and rocks around.

bull's-eye
A **bull's-eye** is the center of a target.

bully
(bullies)
A **bully** is someone who is mean and hurts or frightens others.

bunny
(bunnies)
A **bunny** is a soft furry rabbit with long ears. A **bunny** uses its back legs to hop.

bus
(buses)
A **bus** is a big vehicle that carries a lot of people from place to place. A **bus** has lots of seats and windows but just one driver.

busy
(busier, busiest)
If you are **busy,** you have many things you must do.

but
But means if only or except. *The girl liked every vegetable **but** turnips.*

butter
Butter is a light-yellow food made from cream from a cow. You can cook with it or spread soft **butter** on toast.

butterfly
(butterflies)
A **butterfly** is an insect with big colorful wings. Caterpillars grow up to be **butterflies.**

button
A **button** is a small, round thing that helps to keep your clothes together.

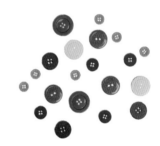

buy
(buys, bought, buying)
When you **buy** something, you pay money for it so you can own it.

by
By means next to. *The boy sits **by** his dog.*

A B C D E F G H I J K L M N O P Q R S T U V W X Y Z

cabbage
A **cabbage** is a vegetable that grows into a head of leaves.

cactus
(cacti)
A **cactus** is a thorny plant that grows in the desert. A **cactus** needs very little water to live.

cage
A **cage** is a room or box with bars where you can keep an animal.

cake
A **cake** is made by baking a mixture of flour, sugar, eggs, and milk in the oven. You put candles on a birthday **cake.**

calculator
People do number problems on a machine called a **calculator.**

calendar
A **calendar** shows the days, weeks, and months of the year. People mark important dates on a **calendar.**

calf
A **calf** is a young cow or bull.

call
(calls, called, calling)
1. If you **call** someone, you can talk to them on the phone. 2. When you **call** out to someone, you speak loudly and want them to come over to you.

camera
You can take photographs with a **camera.**

camp
(camps, camped, camping)
When you **camp,** you live in a tent outdoors for a short time.

can

1. **Can** means you are able to do something. *They **can** jump very high.*
2. A **can** is made of metal and opens on one end. A **can** holds foods and drinks, such as soda.

candle

A **candle** is a piece of wax with a string inside for a wick. When you light the wick, the **candle** burns brightly.

candy

(candies)
Candy is a tasty sweet food made with sugar. Some **candy** is soft, while other **candy** is hard and crunchy.

cane

A **cane** is a curved stick with a handle at the top. Some people use a **cane** to help them walk.

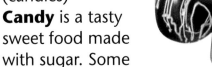

cannot

Cannot means you are unable to do something. *You **cannot** eat a table!*

canteen

A **canteen** is a type of bottle you carry with you on a hike. You drink from your **canteen** when you are thirsty.

cap

1. A **cap** is a soft hat with a round part at the front to shade your eyes. 2. A **cap** is a small lid, like the one on toothpaste.

car

A **car** is a machine with an engine and four wheels that people ride in. You drive a **car** on a road.

card

1. At special times, like a birthday, you send people a **card** with words and pictures. 2. You can play a game with paper **cards** that have numbers, pictures, or words.

care

(cares, cared, caring)
If you **care** about something or someone, you may worry and look after them. *After her brother cut his hand, the girl took **care** of him.*

careful

If you are **careful,** you think about what you are doing so you will do it as well as possible.

carnation

A **carnation** is a fluffy flower that has a sweet, spicy smell.

carrot

A **carrot** is a long, crunchy orange vegetable that grows underground.

carry

(carries, carried, carrying)
When you **carry** something, you pick it up and take it with you.

cart

A **cart** has wheels and a handle. People use a **cart** to carry or push many items or heavy things from place to place.

cash

Cash is money. **Cash** can be coins or paper bills. You use **cash** to buy things.

cashew

A **cashew** is a tan chewy nut that has a shape like a kidney bean.

cassette

A **cassette** is a flat plastic case with a tape inside that records and plays sounds, music, and pictures.

castle

A **castle** is a big, strong stone building with thick walls and towers. Long ago, a **castle** kept the king, queen, and other people who lived inside safe from attackers.

cat

A **cat** is a furry animal with a tail. Small **cats** live in peoples' houses as pets. Large **cats,** like lions and tigers, live in the wild.

catch

(catches, caught, catching)
1. When you get a hold of something that's moving, like a ball, you **catch** it. 2. If you **catch** an illness, you become sick.

26

caterpillar

A **caterpillar** is small and long, like a worm, with little legs. A **caterpillar** changes into a moth or butterfly.

cave

A **cave** is a large hole in the side of a mountain or under the ground.

celery

People eat the crunchy stem of **celery,** a green vegetable.

cellular phone

A **cellular phone** is a telephone without a cord. You can carry a **cellular phone** in your pocket or car.

cent

A **cent** is a very small amount of money. A penny is worth one **cent,** a quarter is worth 25 **cents,** and a dollar is worth 100 **cents.**

cereal

Cereal is a breakfast food usually made out of corn, wheat, or oats and served with milk.

certain

If you are **certain** about something, you are sure of it. *The boy makes **certain** he brushes his teeth right after breakfast.*

chain

Metal rings join together to make a **chain.** A **chain** is used to hold two things together.

chair

A **chair** is a seat with a back for one person to sit on.

chalk

Chalk, made from a soft rock, comes in white and colored sticks. You can draw or write with **chalk** on a chalkboard.

chalkboard

A **chalkboard** is a hard, dark board used for writing with chalk.

chase

(chases, chased, chasing)
If you **chase** something, you run after it and try to catch it.

A B C D E F G H I J K L M N O P Q R S T U V W X Y Z

checkers

In the game of **checkers,** you move flat, round, red or black pieces around a checkered board.

cheese

Cheese is a yellow or white food made from milk. You might eat **cheese** on pizza or in a sandwich.

chef

A **chef** cooks food in a restaurant. A **chef** often wears a tall white hat.

cherry

(cherries)
A **cherry** is a small red fruit with a pit inside. **Cherries** grow on trees, where birds like to eat them.

chess

Chess is a board game for two players. To win at **chess,** you must capture the other player's king.

chest

1. A **chest** is a big heavy box with a lid to store special things inside. 2. Your **chest** is the front part of your body below your neck and between your arms.

chew

(chews, chewed, chewing)
When you **chew** your food, your teeth bite it into small pieces.

chick

A **chick** is a young chicken or other bird. A **chick** makes a *peep-peep* sound.

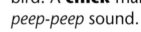

chicken

A **chicken** is a bird that farmers raise for eggs and meat to eat.

child

(children)
A **child** is a young boy or girl. When **children** grow up they become men and women.

28

chimpanzee

A **chimpanzee** is a hairy type of ape that is smaller than a gorilla.

chin

Your **chin** is the part of your face that is below your mouth.

chocolate

Chocolate is a sweet brown food used in candy, cakes, and drinks. **Chocolate** comes from the brown beans of the cocoa tree.

Christmas

Christmas is a holiday on December 25 to celebrate the birth of Christ. People give gifts to each other on **Christmas.**

Christmas tree

People decorate a **Christmas tree** with special pretty things, lights, and ornaments. They put gifts under the **Christmas tree.**

church

(churches)
A **church** is a building where people go to pray and worship.

circle

A **circle** is a round shape like a ring.

circus

(circuses)
A **circus** is a group of people, such as clowns and acrobats, and animals, such as elephants and tigers, that travels around and performs shows.

city

(cities)
A **city** is a very big town where many people work and live.

clam

A **clam** is an ocean animal with a very hard shell that opens and closes. People eat the soft meat inside the **clam.**

clap

(claps, clapped, clapping)
When you **clap,** both of your hands hit together to make a noise.

clarinet

A **clarinet** is a long musical instrument you blow into to make sound. You change the sounds on the **clarinet** with the keys and finger holes.

class

(classes)
A **class** is a group of students learning together.

clay

Clay is soft earth. People make things from **clay,** like bricks, pots, and cups.

clean

(cleans, cleaned, cleaning)
When you **clean** something, you get rid of the dirt.

climb

(climbs, climbed, climbing)
If you **climb,** you move up something tall, like a ladder, using your hands and feet to hold on.

clock

A **clock** is a machine with numbers that tells the time. The short hand on the **clock** tells the hour, and the long hand tells the minutes.

close

(closes, closed, closing)
1. When you **close** something, you shut it. 2. If you stand near someone, you are very **close** to them.

clothes

Clothes are the things you wear, like pants or a shirt. **Clothes,** like a coat, cover your skin and keep you warm.

clothespin

A **clothespin** is a type of wooden or plastic clip that you use to hang wet clothes on the line to dry.

cloud

A **cloud** is a white or gray shape that floats in the sky. **Clouds** are made of many tiny drops of water. Rain falls from dark **clouds.**

clown

A **clown** is a person who dresses up funny and does silly things to make you laugh. Sometimes you see a **clown** at the circus.

club

1. A **club** is a wooden stick, like a bat or golf **club,** used to hit things. 2. A **club** is a group of people who meet for a common interest.

coach

(coaches)
A **coach** is a person who trains and manages players on a sports team, such as baseball.

coat
A **coat** is an article of clothing you wear over your other clothes to keep warm when you go outdoors.

cobra
A **cobra** is a poisonous snake that can flatten the skin on its neck to look like a hood.

cockroach
(cockroaches)
A **cockroach** is a kind of insect with a flat, small body that can squeeze through cracks. Most **cockroaches** come out at night and live in people's houses.

cocoa
Chocolate comes from the brown beans of the **cocoa** tree. People like to drink sweetened hot **cocoa.**

coconut
A **coconut** is a large, brown, round, hard-shelled nut that grows on the **coconut** tree. People eat the chewy white fruit inside a **coconut.**

coffee
Coffee is a brown drink made by adding water to the roasted beans of the **coffee** plant.

coin
A **coin** is a small, round piece of money made from metal. Pennies, nickels, dimes, and quarters are **coins.**

cold
(colder, coldest)
1. If you have a **cold,** you are sick and sneeze or cough a lot. 2. Snow and ice feel **cold** because they are not hot.

color
Color is a way to describe how something looks. *A rainbow has many different **colors,** like red, orange, and yellow.*

colt
A **colt** is a young male horse.

comb
A **comb** is a thing you use to smooth out your hair. A **comb** is flat and hard with long pointed teeth.

come
(comes, came, coming)
1. When you **come,** you move forward toward something. 2. If you want to know when the train will arrive, you ask when it will **come.**

compact disc

A **compact disc**, also called a CD, is a shiny, flat, round piece of plastic with electronic information stored on it. People use **compact discs** to play music and computer games.

compass

(compasses)
So you won't get lost, a **compass** has a needle that shows direction by pointing north.

computer

A **computer** is a machine that stores information and sends messages.

convertible

A **convertible** is a car with a special top that can come off or fold down.

cook

(cooks, cooked, cooking)
When you **cook,** you make or heat food so it is ready to eat. 2. A **cook** is a person who makes or heats food to eat.

cookie

A **cookie** is a small, sweet cake that is baked in the oven. **Cookies** are flat and can be crispy or chewy.

cool

(cooler, coolest)
If something feels **cool,** it is a bit cold.

corn

Farmers grow **corn,** a plant with tall stalks and yellow seed kernels inside ears. You eat **corn** on the cob, and you can pop seeds of **corn** to make popcorn.

cost

(costs, cost, costing)
How much you pay for something is how much it **costs.**

costume

A **costume** is a special set of clothes that an actor or a child wears to pretend to be someone else.

couch

(couches)
A **couch** is a long piece of furniture that is soft to sit on.

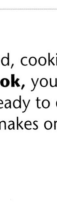

could

Could means you are able to do something. *If you are hot, you **could** get cool in the pool.*

count

(counts, counted, counting)
When you **count,** you say the numbers in the right order: 1, 2, 3.

country

(countries)
1. A **country** is a part of the world with its own name, people, and laws, such as the United States of America or Canada.
2. The **country** is the land outside of towns with fields or woods.

cover

(covers, covered, covering)
1. If you **cover** a thing, you put something over it to keep it warm. *Cover the horse with a blanket so it won't be cold.* 2. A **cover** can hide something. *Put a **cover** over the baby to play peek-a-boo.*

cow

A **cow** is a large farm animal that eats grass and moos. Some **cows** give milk.

cowboy

A **cowboy** or cowgirl lives on a ranch, rides a horse, and takes care of cows.

crab

A **crab** is an ocean animal with a hard shell and sharp pinching claws.

cracker

A **cracker** is a thin, crispy cookie or biscuit.

crawl

(crawls, crawled, crawling)
When you **crawl,** you move along on your hands and knees.

crayon

A **crayon** is a waxy type of colored pencil for drawing.

crib

A **crib** is a bed with tall sides so a baby won't fall out.

cricket

A **cricket** is a jumping insect that makes chirping sounds with its wings.

crocodile

A **crocodile** is a large animal with a long tail and big sharp teeth. A **crocodile** lives in rivers and swamps in some hot places.

cross

(crosses, crossed, crossing)
1. To go from one side to the other means to **cross** over. 2. A **cross** is a mark like a plus (+) or an *x*. 3. If you feel **cross,** you are angry about something.

crown

A **crown** is a beautiful ring of silver or gold and jewels that a king or queen wears on the head.

crutch

(crutches)
A **crutch** is a long sturdy stick that fits under your arm to help you walk if your leg or foot is hurt.

cry

(cries, cried, crying)
You **cry** if you are sad or hurt and tears fall from your eyes.

cub

A **cub** is a baby animal. Baby bears, foxes, wolves, lions, and tigers are cubs.

cup

A **cup** is a container for drinks. A **cup** has a handle.

cupcake

A **cupcake** is a small tasty cake you bake in the oven. Some **cupcakes** are spread with sweet icing.

curtain

A **curtain** is a long piece of fabric that covers a window.

cut

(cuts, cut, cutting)
You can use a sharp knife or scissors to **cut** something into pieces.

cute

(cuter, cutest)
If something looks **cute,** it is pretty.

daisy
(daisies)
A **daisy** is a flower with a yellow center and white petals.

dam
A **dam** is something placed across a river or lake to hold back the water.

dance
(dances, danced, dancing)
When you **dance,** you move your body and feet in time with music.

dandelion
A bright yellow flower, the **dandelion** grows in fields and on lawns.

danger
When there is **danger,** something bad could happen to you.

dark
(darker, darkest)
Dark means something isn't light. The night is **dark.**

daughter
Somebody's **daughter** is a girl who is that person's child.

day
1. **Day** is a time when it is light outside.
2. A **day** is 24 hours long—from one midnight to the next.

dead
If a plant or animal is **dead,** it is not living anymore.

dear
1. You use the word **dear** when you begin writing a letter. 2. If something or somebody is **dear** to you, they are very important.

December
December is the last month of the year. **December** is in the winter.

A B C D E F G H I J K L M N O P Q R S T U V W X Y Z

decide

(decides, decided, deciding)
When you **decide,** you make up your mind about something.

deep

(deeper, deepest)
Something that is **deep** goes a long way down.

deer

(deer)
A **deer** is a big forest animal with short brown fur and long legs for running fast. The male **deer** has big horns on its head called antlers.

desk

A **desk** is a type of table with drawers where you can write or use your computer.

dessert

A **dessert** is a sweet treat, like cake or fruit, that you eat at the end of a meal.

diaper

A **diaper** is underwear for babies made out of cloth or a soft paperlike material.

diary

(diaries)
A **diary** is a blank book in which you write about what is happening to you.

dice

Dice are little cubes with a different number of dots on each side. You roll **dice** when you play some board games. If you only have one of these cubes, it is called a **die.**

dictionary

(dictionaries)
A **dictionary** is a book that tells you what words mean and how to spell them.

different

Different means not the same. *The girls have **different** color hair—one has black hair, the other has red.*

dig

(digs, dug, digging)
If you **dig,** you make a hole in the ground by removing the dirt.

dime

A **dime** is a small, shiny, round metal coin. A **dime** is worth ten cents.

dine

(dines, dined, dining)
When you **dine,** you eat a meal.

dinner

Dinner is the biggest meal of the day. Many people eat their **dinner** at night.

dinosaur

A **dinosaur** is an animal that lived a long, long time ago. Some **dinosaurs,** such as *Tyrannosaurus rex,* were giants.

dip

(dips, dipped, dipping)
If you **dip** something, you place it in a liquid and then quickly pull it out.

direction

A **direction** is the way a person is facing or pointing.

dirt

Dirt is mud or soil that makes something unclean.

discover

(discovers, discovered, discovering)
When you **discover** something, you are learning about it for the first time.

dish

(dishes)
A **dish** is something you put food on or in when you eat.
Plates and bowls are types of **dishes.**

dive

(dives, dived, diving)
When you **dive** into the water, you jump in with your arms and head first.

A B C D E F G H I J K L M N O P Q R S T U V W X Y Z

A B C D E F G H I J K L M N O P Q R S T U V W X Y Z

divide

(divides, divided, dividing)
When you **divide** something, you make it into smaller parts.

do

(does, did, done, doing)
When you **do** something, you make something or you make something happen. *When you draw a card for Mommy, you **do** it all by yourself.*

doctor

A **doctor** is someone who helps sick people get better.

dog

A **dog** is a furry animal that barks. Some **dogs** live in a house as a pet, while others do work, like guarding buildings or farm animals.

doll

A **doll** is a small toy that can look like a child or an adult.

dollar

A kind of money, a **dollar** looks like a piece of green paper. One **dollar** is worth 100 cents, the same as 100 pennies or 4 quarters.

dolphin

A **dolphin** is a big, smart animal that lives in the ocean. A **dolphin** is not a fish. A **dolphin** blows air through a hole in its back.

donkey

A **donkey** is an animal that looks like a small horse with long ears.

door

You open a **door** when you need to go into a room or building, and you close the **door** behind you when you leave.

doorbell

You push the button on a **doorbell,** and it rings or buzzes to let people inside the building know you want to come in.

dot
A **dot** is a very small round spot.

doubt
(doubts, doubted, doubting)
If you **doubt** something, you are not sure about it, or you question it. *You might **doubt** that you can swim all the way across the pool.*

doughnut
A **doughnut** is a round, sweet cake with a hole in the middle.

down
Down is the direction something takes to move from a higher place to a lower one. *The ball rolls **down** the hill.*

dozen
A **dozen** is a group of 12 things, like a **dozen** eggs in a box.

dragon
A **dragon** is a huge make-believe monster with scales, wings, a long tail, and fiery breath. **Dragons** appear in many stories.

draw
(draws, drew, drawing)
When you **draw,** you make a picture with a pencil, a pen, or crayons.

drawing
A **drawing** is a picture you make with a pencil, a pen, or crayons.

dream
(dreams, dreamed, dreaming)
When you **dream,** pictures and thoughts go through your mind after you are asleep.

dress
(dresses, dressed, dressing)
1. When you **dress,** you put your clothes on. 2. A **dress** is a skirt and top sewn together for girls to wear.

dresser
A **dresser** is a piece of furniture with many drawers to hold clothes.

drill

A **drill** is a tool with a sharp point that makes small holes in metal or wood by turning that point.

drink

(drinks, drank, drinking)
1. When you pour a liquid, like juice, into your mouth and swallow it, you are **drinking.** 2. A **drink** is a liquid, such as water, that you swallow when you are thirsty.

drive

(drives, drove, driven, driving)
1. When you ride in a car or bus, you are going for a **drive.** 2. When you **drive** a car or bus, you make it move along the road.

drop

(drops, dropped, dropping)
1. If you **drop** something, you let it fall. 2. A **drop** is a very small amount of liquid, like a **drop** of rain.

drum

A **drum** is a round, hollow musical instrument that you can tap with sticks or your hands.

dry

(dries, dried, drying, drier, driest)
1. When you **dry** something, like rubbing it with a towel, you take the water off of it. 2. Something that is **dry** is not wet.

duck

A **duck** is a bird that swims in the water with its webbed feet and flies in the air with its wings. A **duck** makes a quacking sound.

duckling

A **duckling** is a baby duck. **Ducklings** have soft fluffy feathers and walk and swim in line behind their mother.

during

During means through the time of. *The children listened **during** the story.*

each

Each means every thing or every person. *The father gave **each** one of his children a cupcake for a snack.*

eagle

An **eagle** is a large bird with a sharp curved beak and long wings. An **eagle** catches other birds.

ear

An **ear** is the part of your body that you use to hear. You have one **ear** on each side of your head.

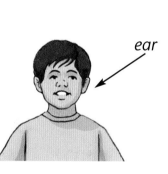

ear

early

(earlier, earliest)
Early means before something starts. If you arrive **early,** you get somewhere sooner than you expected.

earth

1. We live on the planet **Earth,** which includes all of the oceans and land.
2. You can plant things in the **earth,** or ground.

east

The direction in which the sun comes up in the morning is **east.**

Easter

Easter is a special Christian holiday that occurs in the spring. Children enjoy hunting for colored **Easter** eggs during the **Easter** holiday.

easy

(easier, easiest)
If something is **easy,** it is not very hard for someone to do.

eat

(eats, ate, eaten, eating)
When you **eat,** you place food in your mouth, chew it, and then swallow it.

edge

The **edge** is the part along the side or end of something. *The doll sits on the **edge** of the chair.*

egg

An **egg** is a smooth round object that may have a baby bird, fish, reptile, or insect growing inside of it. Chickens lay **eggs** with a hard shell. Some people cook and eat **eggs.**

eight

Eight is a number that is one more than seven.

eighteen

Eighteen is a number that is one more than seventeen. 17+1=18.

eighty

Eighty is eight groups of 10. 8×10=80.

elephant

An **elephant** is the largest land animal. An **elephant** is gray with a long nose called a trunk and two huge ears.

eleven

Eleven is a number that is one more than ten.

empty

(emptier, emptiest)
When something is **empty,** it has nothing inside.

end

The last part of something is the **end.** *You are finished listening to the CD now that you are at the* **end.**

English

English is the main language spoken in the United States, Canada, England, and some other countries.

enough

If you have **enough** of something, you have as much as you need. *When you eat until you are full, you have had* **enough** *to eat.*

enter

(enters, entered, entering)
You go into a place when you **enter** it.

envelope

An **envelope** is a folded paper cover for a letter that you glue shut. On the front of an **envelope,** you place a stamp and write the address.

erase
(erases, erased, erasing)
When you **erase** something, you wipe it out so it can no longer be seen.

eraser
When you rub with an **eraser,** it wipes away pencil marks from paper. Some pencils have a small **eraser** on the end.

escape
(escapes, escaped, escaping)
When you **escape,** you get away from something.

even
1. An **even** number is one that you can divide by two. The opposite of an **even** number (2, 4 . . .) is an odd number (3, 5 . . .).
2. If something is flat or level, like a floor, it is **even.**

evening
Evening is the part of day between afternoon and night. The sun goes down in the **evening.**

ever
1. **Ever** means for all time. *At the end of the story, the man and woman lived happily **ever** after.* 2. **Ever** means at any time at all. *Have you **ever** played soccer?*

every
Every means each of a group without exception. *You must pick up **every** toy from the floor.*

except
Except means someone or something is left out. *Everyone **except** the baby, who is too young, went to the movies.*

exercise
(exercises, exercised, exercising)
1. When you **exercise,** you do an activity to develop or improve your body. *We **exercise** our legs by running.*

2. An **exercise** is a small bit of work you do to help you learn something. *You can practice an **exercise** on your piano.*

extra
Extra means more of something than usual. *Would you like to eat an **extra** scoop of ice cream?*

eye
Your **eye** is the part of your face you use to see.

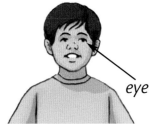

eye

face

Your **face** is the front part of your head. Your eyes, nose, and mouth are on your **face.**

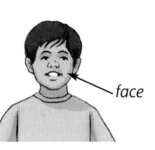

face

fair

(fairer, fairest)
1. If you are honest and follow the rules, you are playing **fair.** 2. **Fair** means light in color. *The baby's skin is **fair** because he has not been out in the sun.* 3. A **fair** is a special place where you have fun on big rides, play games for prizes, and see farm foods and animals.

falcon

A **falcon** is a bird with powerful wings, good eyes, and a pointed beak. A **falcon** is a good hunter.

fall

(falls, fell, fallen, falling)
1. If something **falls,** it suddenly goes down toward the ground. 2. **Fall** is the season of the year between summer and winter.

family

(families)
A **family** is a group of related people, such as children, parents, and grandparents.

fan

1. A **fan** is an object that moves or blows air around to make you feel cool. 2. A **fan** is a person who admires someone else's skills. *The **fans** cheer when the player catches the baseball.*

far

(farther, farthest)
Far means a long way. *The moon is **far** away from Earth.*

farm

A **farm** is a piece of land where a farmer grows food and raises animals.

farmer

A **farmer** is a person who works on a farm taking care of the animals and the crops.

fast

(faster, fastest)
If someone or something moves along quickly, that person or thing goes **fast.**

fat

(fatter, fattest)
A **fat** animal or person has a big, round body.

father

A **father** is a man who has a child.

fear

Fear is when you feel afraid of someone or something. *You have a **fear** of getting burned if you touch the hot oven.*

feather

Birds have **feathers** to cover their skin. **Feathers** are soft and very light.

February

February is a winter month and the second month of the year. *Valentine's Day is in **February.***

feed

(feeds, fed, feeding)
When you **feed** someone or something, you give that person or thing food to eat.

feel

(feels, felt, feeling)
1. You can touch something to see what it **feels** like. 2. When you **feel** sad or sick, that is how you are at the time. *The little girl **feels** happy because her daddy gave her balloons.*

feet

1. You have two **feet** on the end of your legs. You stand on your **feet**. 2. Feet are a measurement. There are three **feet** in one yard.

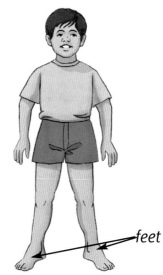

feet

fence

A **fence** is a kind of outside wall made of wood or metal. A **fence** around a farm keeps the animals in.

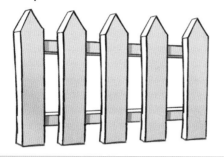

few

(fewer, fewest)
Few means not very many. *Only a **few** caterpillars turned into butterflies.*

fib

(fibs, fibbed, fibbing)
When someone **fibs,** he is saying a little lie or untruth.

fifteen

Fifteen is a number that is one more than fourteen.10+5=15.

fifth

Fifth means something that is number five in a series that you count. *The black dog is the **fifth** one in the line.*

fifty

Fifty is a number that means five groups of ten. 10+10+10+10+10=50.

fight

(fights, fought, fighting)
When people or animals **fight,** they try to hurt one another. *When the boys **fight,** they hit each other with their hands.*

fill

(fills, filled, filling)
When you **fill** something, you put in so much that there is not room for any more. *Your sister **fills** her glass right up to the top with orange juice.*

find

(finds, found, finding)
When you **find** something, you see something that was lost. *The baby **finds** his toy under the chair.*

fine

Fine means something is very good. *You look **fine** in your pretty new party dress.*

finger

Your **fingers** are the five long, thin parts at the end of your hand. Your **fingers** bend so you can pick up things. Your thumb is one of your **fingers.**

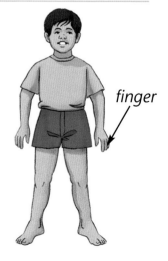

finger

A
B
C
D
E
F
G
H
I
J
K
L
M
N
O
P
Q
R
S
T
U
V
W
X
Y
Z

finish
(finishes, finished, finishing)
When you **finish** something, you come to the end of it. *When daddy **finishes** reading his book, he closes it.*

fire
Fire is the hot, bright light that happens when something burns. A **fire** keeps you warm.

firefighter
A **firefighter** is a person who puts out a fire with water from a hose. **Firefighters** wear heavy boots and helmets so they don't get burned.

fire truck
Firefighters ride to put out a fire on a **fire truck. Fire trucks** carry hoses and ladders.

first
1. **First** means at the front or at the beginning. When you win a race, you come in **first.** 2. **First** is number one in a series you count.

fish
(fishes, fished, fishing)
1. When you **fish,** you use a net or fishing pole to catch the **fish.** 2. A **fish** is an animal with scales that lives under water. A **fish** uses its fins and tail to swim.

fishing pole
A **fishing pole** is a long stick with a string and a hook used to catch fish.

fit
(fits, fit, fitting)
1. If something **fits** you, it is just the right size. *Cinderella's shoe **fit** her foot perfectly.* 2. If you are strong, healthy, and in good shape, you are **fit.** *Mommy exercises to stay **fit.***

five
Five is a number that is one more than four.

fix
(fixes, fixed, fixing)
When you **fix** something, you repair it or put it back together again.

flag

A **flag** is a piece of cloth you hang up with colored shapes or letters on it. Every country has its own **flag.**

flashlight

A **flashlight** is a small lamp you can hold in your hand to light up dark places.

flippers

Flippers are wide, flat shoes that can help you swim faster. A duck's webbed feet are **flippers.**

float

(floats, floated, floating)
1. When something stays on top of the water, it **floats.** *A toy boat **floats** in the bathtub.* 2. If something **floats** in the air, it moves slowly along without falling down. *The balloon **floats** toward the tall trees.*

floor

The **floor** is the bottom part of a room. You walk on the **floor.**

flower

The **flower** is the part of a plant that has colored petals and smells good.

flute

A **flute** is a musical instrument that works like a whistle. You blow air into the **flute** and use the keys and finger holes to change sounds.

fly

(flies, flew, flown, flying)
1. When something **flies,** it moves through the air. A bird **flies** from tree to tree. 2. A **fly** is a small insect with wings that makes a buzzing sound.

fold

(folds, folded, folding)
When you **fold** something, you bend parts over each other. *After you **fold** the shirts, you put them in the basket.*

folder

A cardboard **folder** holds important papers from school or work.

A B C D E F G H I J K L M N O P Q R S T U V W X Y Z

follow
(follows, following, followed)
When you **follow** someone or something, you are moving along right behind that person or thing.

food
Food is all of the things that plants, animals, and people eat to stay healthy.

foot
(feet)
1. Your **foot** is the part of your body at the end of your leg. You stand on your **feet.** 2. A **foot** is a measurement. Twelve inches equals a **foot** on a ruler.

foot

football
1. A **football** is a ball that is round in the middle and pointed at the ends.
2. When you play the game of **football,** two teams throw, catch, and kick a **football** to score points.

footprint
A **footprint** is the mark a foot leaves in the ground.

for
For is used to show how something is used or where something goes. *A crayon is **for** drawing. The baker made the birthday cake **for** you.*

forest
A **forest** is a place where many trees grow together.

forget
(forgets, forgot, forgotten, forgetting)
If you **forget** something, you do not remember it. *I **forgot** to return my library book. He **forgot** the name of that person.*

fork
A **fork** is a tool with a handle and several sharp points at the end. You use a **fork** to pick up food and eat.

forty
Forty is a number that is four groups of ten. 10+10+10+10=40.

four

Four is a number that is one more than three. *A horse has **four** legs.*

fourteen

Fourteen is a number that is one less than fifteen.

fourth

Fourth means one that is number four in a series that you count. *The chocolate scoop is the **fourth** one in the cone.*

fox

(foxes)

A **fox** is a wild, furry animal that has pointy ears and a long, bushy tail. A **fox** is smaller than most dogs.

frame

A **frame** is a border around a picture.

freckle

A **freckle** is a small brown spot on your skin.

free

(freer, freest)

1. If something is **free,** there is no charge and you do not pay for it. 2. When something is **free** or loose, it can go anywhere.

French

French is a language that is spoken in France, Canada, and other countries.

Friday

Friday is the day of the week that comes after Thursday.

friend

A **friend** is a person who you know very well and like a great deal.

frog

A **frog** is a small animal that leaps on land and swims in the water with its strong back legs. **Frogs** eat flies.

from

From is used to show a starting point. *The girl is coming **from** school to home.*

front

The part that comes first or you see first is the **front.** *The front of a book is the cover.*

frown

(frowns, frowned, frowning)
When you **frown,** your face wrinkles to show you are mad or sad.

fruit

The **fruit** is the part of the plant that has seeds in it. We like to eat **fruits,** such as apples and blueberries.

fry

(fries, fried, frying)
When you **fry** foods, you cook them in oil in a pan on the stove.

full

(fuller, fullest)
If something is **full,** it cannot hold any more. *I cannot eat more pizza because my tummy is full.*

fun

When you are having **fun,** you are having a good time and enjoying yourself.

funny

(funnier, funniest)
1. If something is **funny,** it makes you laugh. 2. When something is acting **funny,** it appears to be strange. *The alarm clock makes a very funny sound.*

fur

Fur is soft, thick hair that covers many animals, such as dogs, bears, and lions.

furniture

Furniture is something that people use in their homes to sit on, eat on, sleep on, and work on. Chairs, tables, beds, and desks are types of **furniture.**

furry

(furrier, furriest)
Something that is **furry** is all covered with a thick, soft coat of hair. Kittens and bunnies are **furry.**

A B C D E F G H I J K L M N O P Q R S T U V W X Y Z

game

A **game** is something with rules that you play for fun. Basketball and chess are **games.**

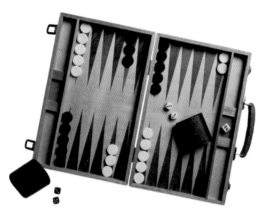

garage

A **garage** is a place where cars get fixed and gas is sometimes sold. A **garage** can also be a part of a building or house where cars are kept.

garbage

Garbage is all the things you throw away. People put **garbage** in large bags or cans, but it may still get smelly.

garden

A **garden** is a piece of land near your home where you grow flowers and vegetables.

garlic

Garlic is a plant that grows in bulbs. People like to cook with strong-smelling **garlic.**

gas

(gases)

People go to the gas station to put **gas** in their cars and trucks. Liquid **gas** burns inside the car's engine to make it go.

gate

A **gate** is like a door in a fence or a wall. *When the **gate** is open, you can drive the tractor to the barn.*

gerbil

A small furry animal, a **gerbil** has long back legs and a thin tail. Some **gerbils** are pets.

get

(gets, got, gotten, getting)
When you **get** something, you obtain it. *If you are hungry, you need to **get** some breakfast.*

ghost

In stories, a **ghost** is the spirit of a person who has died. *You might dress up like a scary **ghost** for Halloween.*

giant

A **giant** is a very big person that you can read about in storybooks.

gift

A **gift** is something special that you give to someone. You might wrap a **gift** with colored paper and a bow.

giraffe

A **giraffe** is a wild African animal with a very long neck, long legs, and brown spots. **Giraffes** eat leaves from tall trees.

girl

A **girl** is a female child who will grow up to be a woman.

give

(gives, gave, given, giving)
If you **give** another person something, you let him or her have it. ***Give** your friend the bat so she can play baseball.*

glad

If you are **glad,** you are happy about something. *I'm **glad** the sun is shining.*

glass

(glasses)
1. **Glass** is a hard, smooth material that you can see through, such as a window.
2. A **glass** is something you drink from. In a clear **glass,** you can see liquids such as water, milk, and juice.

glasses

People wear **glasses** over their eyes to help them see better. **Glasses** are pieces of special glass inside of a frame that fits over the nose.

glider

A **glider** is an aircraft that flies without an engine. The wings of a **glider** help it float through the air.

globe

A **globe** is a big round map of the whole world that spins around.

glove

A **glove** keeps your hand warm and clean. **Gloves** come in pairs and fit over your fingers.

glow

(glows, glowed, glowing)
If something **glows,** it shines with light and color. *The stars **glowed** brightly in the night sky.*

glue

Glue is a thick liquid that helps stick things together. **Glue** gets hard when it dries.

go

(goes, went, gone, going)
When you **go,** you move from one place to another. *The train is **going** down the track.*

goat

A **goat** is a farm animal with short horns. Farmers raise **goats** for their wool and milk.

goggles

Goggles are a special type of clear glasses made to protect the eyes. Swimmers and carpenters sometimes wear **goggles.**

gold

Gold is a shiny yellow metal used to make jewelry and coins.

goldfish
(goldfish)
A **goldfish** is a small fish that people keep as a pet.

golf
You play the game of **golf** by hitting a little white ball into a hole with a club. A person who plays **golf** is a golfer.

gone
If someone is **gone,** he or she has moved on to another place. *The boy was here, but now he is **gone.***

good
(better, best)
1. You are **good** at something you do well. 2. If something tastes really **good,** you will like it. 3. You become healthy or strong if you eat something **good** for you. 4. If you are well behaved and do as you are told, you are **good.**

good-bye
You say **good-bye** when you leave someone or they go away from you.

goose
(geese)
A **goose** is a big bird with a long neck that swims well. Some **geese** fly south where it is warm for the winter.

gorilla
A **gorilla** is a large, hairy ape that lives in Africa.

grade
1. A **grade** is something you earn while learning. A teacher marks your paper with a **grade,** such as a "happy face."
2. A **grade** is the level where a student is in school. *The twins are in second **grade.***

grandfather
Your **grandfather** is the father of your mother or father.

grandmother
Your **grandmother** is the mother of your mother or father.

grape
A **grape** is a small, round, soft, juicy fruit that grows in bunches on vines. **Grapes** can be purple, green, or white.

grapefruit
(grapefruit)

A **grapefruit** is a large, round fruit, similar to an orange, with a thick yellow or pinkish skin. The soft inside of a **grapefruit** tastes tangy sweet.

grass
(grasses)

Grass is a plant with thin, pointy green leaves. **Grass** grows on lawns and fields.

grasshopper

A **grasshopper** is a large, green, leaping, plant-eating insect.

gray

When you mix black and white together, you make the color **gray.** *An elephant is gray.*

great
(greater, greatest)

1. **Great** means that someone is very important. *Abraham Lincoln was a great president.* 2. **Great** means big. *There is a great amount of water in the ocean.* 3. **Great** means something is very good. *She had a great time in the park.*

green

If you mix yellow and blue together, you make the color **green.** *Grass is green.*

green bean

A **green bean** is a long, thin vegetable.

grin
(grins, grinned, grinning)

When you **grin,** you smile and show your teeth.

groceries

Groceries are things that people buy at the store, such as milk, bread, and shampoo.

ground

The **ground** is what you walk on outside.

group

A **group** is a number of people or things that are gathered together in one place. *A group of children visits the zoo.*

A B C D E F G H I J K L M N O P Q R S T U V W X Y Z

grow
(grows, grew, grown, growing)
To **grow** is to get bigger. *If you water the plant, it will **grow.***

grown-up
A **grown-up** is an adult. When a child gets to be older, he or she will become a **grown-up.**

guard
A **guard** watches over people or things to keep them safe. *A security **guard** works at a bank.*

guess
(guesses, guessed, guessing)
When you **guess,** you try to give an answer to something you are not quite sure about. *Can you **guess** how many kittens your cat will have?*

guide
(guides, guided, guiding)
1. If you **guide** someone, you give directions or show that person how to do something. 2. A **guide** is someone who takes people somewhere. *Our **guide** showed us around the museum.*

guitar
A **guitar** is a musical instrument with strings you touch with your fingers to make a sound.

gum
1. **Gum** is a sweetened stick or tablet you put in your mouth and chew.
2. Your **gums** are the soft flesh in your mouth that surround your teeth.

gym
A **gym** is a big room where people like to exercise and play games such as basketball.

hair

Hair grows on the top of your head. An animal's **hair** is called fur.

half

(halves)
One **half** is one of two pieces of something that are exactly the same size. *My father cut the sandwich in **half.***

hall

A **hall** is a large or long room with doors leading to other rooms in a building. *My bedroom is at the end of the **hall.***

Halloween

Halloween is a holiday that happens on October 31. People dress up in costumes and go door-to-door to get **Halloween** candy.

ham

Ham is a pink meat that people like to eat in sandwiches. **Ham** comes from a hog.

hamburger

A **hamburger** is a flat, round piece of chopped beef on a bun. *Many people put ketchup on a **hamburger.***

hammer

A **hammer** is a tool with a long handle and a heavy head. You pound nails into wood with a **hammer** to build things.

hamster

A **hamster** is a small, furry animal that stores food in its puffy cheeks. Some **hamsters** are pets.

hand

(hands, handed, handing)
1. When you **hand** something to somebody, you give it to them with your **hand.** 2. Your **hand** is the part of your body at the end of your arms with four fingers and a thumb.

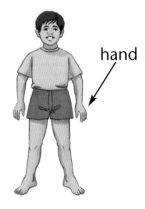

hand

hanger

A **hanger** is a triangular shape made of wood or metal with a hook on the top that holds your clothes.

Hanukkah

Hanukkah is an eight-day Jewish holiday that occurs in the winter. Each night of **Hanukkah,** candles are lit on the menorah. Children play with a dreidel during **Hanukkah.**

happen

(happens, happened, happening)
When something **happens,** it takes place. *The sunrise **happens** every morning.*

happy

(happier, happiest)
If you are **happy,** you feel really good about something. *You are **happy** you won the game of checkers.*

hard

(harder, hardest)
1. If something is **hard,** you cannot easily shape it with your hands or cut it. *A rock is very **hard.*** 2. If something is **hard** to do, it can be difficult. *It is **hard** to learn to tie my shoelaces.*

harmonica

A **harmonica** is a small musical instrument. You blow air through the holes in a **harmonica** with your mouth to make a musical sound.

hat

A **hat** is something you wear on your head.

have

(has, had, having)
1. **Have** means you or other people get or own something. *You **have** a loose tooth.* 2. Have means something must be done. *Now that the children are feeling better, they **have** to go to school today.*

he

He is a word you use when you are talking about a boy, a man, or a male animal of any age.

head

1. Your **head** is the part of your body above your neck that has your eyes and mouth in it. 2. A **head** of something is also a leader. *Your principal is the **head** of your school.*

head

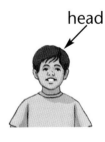

A B C D E F G H I J K L M N O P Q R S T U V W X Y Z

health

If you have your **health,** your body and mind are fine. If you have good **health,** you are not sick.

hear

(hears, heard, hearing)
When you **hear** sounds, you notice them with your ears.

heart

1. Your **heart** is inside your chest and pumps blood to all parts of your body. 2. A **heart** is a shape that people enjoy drawing around Valentine's Day.

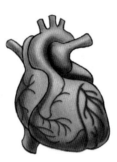

heat

(heats, heated, heating)
When you **heat** something, you make it hot. *Your mom **heats** soup for your lunch.*

heaven

1. For some people, **heaven** means a paradise or the home of God and the angels. 2. The **heavens** are the sky and outer space. *You look up into the **heavens** when the stars are bright at night.*

heavy

(heavier, heaviest)
Something that weighs a lot is **heavy.** *The box of stones is **heavy.***

helicopter

A **helicopter** is a flying machine without wings. A **helicopter** has blades on its top that turn around.

hello

Hello is a way to greet people. You say **"hello"** when you answer your telephone.

helmet

A **helmet** is a hard hat that you wear to protect your head.

help

(helps, helped, helping)
If you **help** someone, you do something useful for them. *You **help** pick up the dishes after dinner.*

helper

You are a **helper** when you assist others. *At school, the **helper** of the day holds the door for everyone.*

hen

A **hen** is a mother chicken, or a female bird that lays eggs.

her

Her means that something is about or belongs to a girl or a woman. *That is her gold necklace.*

here

If you are **here,** you are in or at this certain place. *The kitten is here in the box.*

hero

(heroes)
A **hero** is someone who is admired for being brave. *A firefighter is a hero.*

hers

Hers means something belongs to her, a girl or a woman. *The dress is hers.*

hide

(hides, hid, hidden, hiding)
1. If you **hide,** you go where no one can see you. 2. If you **hide** something, you place it where no one can find it.

high

(higher, highest)
If something is **high,** it is a long way from the ground. *The balloon is high up in the sky.*

high chair

A **high chair** is a tall seat where babies eat. A **high chair** has a tray in front.

hill

A **hill** is a high piece of land.

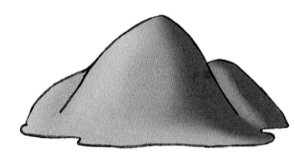

him

Him means that something is about a boy or a man. *The boy asked his mother to give him a quarter.*

hip

Your **hip** is the part of your body on your side just below your waist.

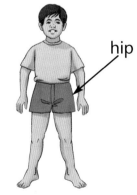

hip

his

His means that something belongs to **him,** a boy or a man. *The toy truck is his.*

A B C D E F G H I J K L M N O P Q R S T U V W X Y Z

hit
(hits, hit, hitting)
When you push or touch someone or something very hard, you **hit** that person or thing.

hockey
Hockey is a game played on ice or in a field with two teams. In ice **hockey,** players on skates try to hit a **hockey** puck with sticks. Field **hockey** players run across the ground and hit a ball with sticks.

hog
A **hog** is a full-grown pig that farmers raise for its meat, such as ham.

hold
(holds, held, holding)
1. When you **hold** something, you have it in your hands. *The boy **holds** the fishing pole.* 2. **Hold** also means to contain or have something inside. *The vase **holds** water and flowers.*

hole
A **hole** is an empty space or a gap. *A bagel has a **hole** in the middle of it.*

holiday
A **holiday** is a special time when people do not go to school or work. People have parades on some **holidays,** such as New Year's Day.

home
A **home** is the place where you live. A home can be a house or an apartment.

homework
Homework is school studies to be done outside of school, usually at home. *The boy is reading a book in his bedroom for **homework.***

honey
Honey is a thick, sweet, liquid food made by bees.

honk
(honks, honked, honking)
Honk means to make loud blasting sound. *Geese and car horns **honk.***

honor

(honors, honored, honoring)
You show respect for someone or something when you **honor** that person or thing. *The man **honored** the flag by flying it.*

hop

(hops, hopped, hopping)
When you **hop,** you jump.

hope

(hopes, hoped, hoping)
If you **hope** something will happen, you want it to and think that it might. *I **hope** I get a bicycle for my birthday.*

horn

1. A **horn** is a brass musical instrument that you blow air into for a sound to come out. 2. A **horn** is a hard, pointed thing that grows out of the heads of some animals, like sheep and bulls.

horrible

If someone or something is **horrible,** that person or thing is terrible or awful. *The burned cookies tasted so **horrible,** I could not eat them.*

horse

A **horse** is a big animal with long legs and a long tail. People like to ride on a **horse** or in a cart pulled behind a **horse.**

horseshoe

1. A **horseshoe** is a heavy U-shaped piece of metal that protects a horse's hoof. 2. In the game of **horseshoes,** you try to throw a horseshoe around a stake.

hose

A **hose** is a bendable tube that liquid flows through. *Firefighters use big **hoses** to spray water on fires.*

A B C D E F G H I J K L M N O P Q R S T U V W X Y Z

hot
(hotter, hottest)
Hot means very warm. If something is **hot,** such as an oven, it can burn you.

hot dog
A **hot dog** is a long piece of meat in a soft roll that you eat. Some people like to put mustard on their **hot dogs.**

hour
An **hour** is an amount of time. There are 60 minutes in one **hour** and 24 **hours** in one day.

house
A **house** is a building where people, often a single family, live.

how
How means in what way or condition. *The doctor might ask, "**How** are you feeling?"*

hug
(hugs, hugged, hugging)
When you put your arms around something or somebody and hold tightly, you are giving a **hug.**

huge
If something is very, very big, it is **huge.** *A dinosaur is a **huge** animal.*

hundred
A **hundred** is a large number meaning 10 groups of 10. *There are one **hundred** pennies in a dollar.*

100

hungry
(hungrier, hungriest)
When you feel **hungry,** you feel like you want to eat something.

hurry
(hurries, hurried, hurrying)
When you **hurry,** you do things quickly.

hurt
(hurts, hurt, hurting)
If you **hurt,** you feel pain. *I fell and **hurt** my hand and my arm.*

husband
A woman's **husband** is the man that she married.

I

I means the person who is speaking. *"I want to play with the toys."*

ice

Ice is hard, cold, frozen water.

ice cream

Ice cream is a cold, sweet food made from milk that comes in many flavors. You can eat **ice cream** in a cone or a dish.

idea

An **idea** is something that you think of. *Do you have an idea how to color Easter eggs?*

if

If means in the event that. *The girl can go to the party if her mother lets her.*

igloo

An **igloo** is a house made of blocks of snow or ice.

ill

When you are **ill,** you do not feel very well. *You should stay in bed when you are ill.*

important

If something is very **important**, it matters a great deal. *It is important to brush your teeth after eating.*

in

In is used to tell about location. *The horse is in the barn.*

inch

(inches)

0   1

An **inch** is a unit of measure that tells about length. *Most rulers have 12 inches.*

insect

An **insect** is a small animal with six legs. Some **insects** can fly. Ants, butterflies, and bees are **insects.**

inside

If you are **inside** of something, it is all around you. *The pear is **inside** the box.*

instead

Instead means in place of something. *I'd rather go by bus **instead** of by train.*

instrument

1. You can use an **instrument** to make music. Pianos, drums, and violins are musical **instruments.** 2. An instrument is anything you use to do something. *At the doctor's office, the doctor used **instruments** to find out why you felt sick.*

into

Into means to go to the inside of something. *Your dog stepped **into** his doghouse.*

iron

1. A hot **iron** is a tool that you use to take wrinkles out of clothes. An **iron** has a handle and a flat side. 2. **Iron** is a very strong metal.

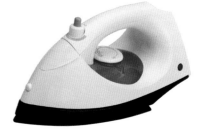

is

(be, am, are, was, were, been, being) **Is** means something or someone exists. *The woman **is** a doctor.*

island

An **island** is a piece of land with water all around it. An **island** is smaller than a continent.

it

1. **It** means that one. *I picked **it** up.* 2. In a game of tag, **it** is the player who tries to catch the others.

its

Its means that it relates to that one. ***Its** tail is black and white.*

jacket

A **jacket** is a short coat. *You wear a jacket when the weather is cool.*

jack-in-the-box

(jack-in-the-boxes)
Music plays when you turn the handle of a **jack-in-the-box.** When the music stops, a doll pops out of the toy **jack-in-the-box.**

jack-o-lantern

A **jack-o-lantern** is a Halloween pumpkin. People carve scary or happy faces on their **jack-o-lanterns.**

jam

(jams, jammed, jamming)
1. If something **jams,** it becomes stuck so it is hard to move. 2. **Jam** is a sweet food made by cooking fruit with sugar. You eat **jam** on your toast.

January

January is the first month of the year. *New Year's Day is in **January.***

jar

A **jar** is a wide-mouth glass bottle that holds things, such as food, liquid, or coins.

jeans

Jeans are pants made out of a strong denim cloth. **Jeans** are usually blue and have pockets.

jelly

(jellies)
Jelly is a soft food made with fruit juice and sugar. *People like to spread **jelly** and peanut butter on bread.*

jelly bean

A **jelly bean** is a small, sweet, chewy, colorful candy.

A B C D E F G H I J K L M N O P Q R S T U V W X Y Z

jet

A **jet** is the fastest kind of airplane. A **jet** has a strong engine.

jewelry

Jewelry is a beautiful decoration that people wear, like rings, earrings, and necklaces.

job

1. A **job** is the work people do to make money. *Daddy has a **job** as a teacher.*
2. A **job** is something that must be done. *My **job** is to set the table.*

joke

A **joke** is something you do or say to make others laugh.

juice

Juice is a liquid that you squeeze from fruits, like oranges and grapes. *Juice is good to drink.*

July

July is the seventh month of the year. **July** is a summer month. *People celebrate the Fourth of **July** with parades and fireworks.*

jump

(jumps, jumped, jumping)
You **jump** when you push yourself up into the air with your legs. *A rabbit **jumps** with its back legs.*

jump rope

A **jump rope** is a toy with two handles and a rope in between. You swing the **jump rope** over your head and jump when it reaches your feet.

June

June is the sixth month of the year. *People graduate or finish school for the summer in **June**.*

jungle

A **jungle** is a thick forest in a hot country where many kinds of plants and animals live.

Jupiter

Jupiter is a faraway planet that moves around the sun. **Jupiter** is the largest planet in the solar system.

kangaroo

A **kangaroo** is a large wild animal that jumps with its strong back legs. A mother **kangaroo** carries her baby in front in a pocket.

keep

(keeps, kept, keeping)
1. If you **keep** something, it is safe and you are not giving it away. 2. If you **keep** doing something, you do it over and over again. *I keep blowing on the soup to make it cool.* 3. **Keep** means to stay the same way. *Keep still so the bee doesn't sting you.*

keeper

A **keeper** cares for someone or something. *An animal keeper watches over the animals.*

ketchup

Ketchup is a thick, red liquid food made from tomatoes. *People pour ketchup from a bottle on top of hamburgers.*

key

A **key** is a piece of metal that you put in a lock to open or close it. *You can open your door with a key.*

kick

(kicks, kicked, kicking)
When you **kick** something, you strike it with your foot.

kid

1. A **kid** is a child. 2. A **kid** is what a young goat is called.

kill

(kills, killed, killing)
To **kill** means to make something or someone die. *You will kill your plant if you don't give it water.*

kind

(kinder, kindest)
1. A **kind** of something means a type or sort of thing. *An apple is a kind of fruit.* 2. If you are a **kind** person, it means you are nice and helpful.

king

A **king** is a man who rules a country. *The **king** and queen rode in the royal carriage.*

kiss

(kisses, kissed, kissing)
When you **kiss** someone, your lips touch that person in a nice way.

kitchen

A **kitchen** is a room where people cook food. A **kitchen** has a stove, a refrigerator, and a sink.

kite

A **kite** is a toy made from sticks, string, and cloth, paper, or plastic that flies in the wind. You hold the string to fly the **kite.**

kitten

A **kitten** is a baby cat with soft fur and little whiskers.

knee

Your **knee** is the part in the middle of your leg that bends.

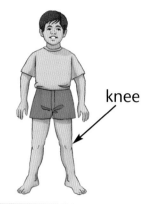

knee

knife

(knives)
A **knife** is a tool with a sharp metal blade and a long handle. *You can cut food into pieces with a **knife.***

knock

(knocks, knocked, knocking)
When you **knock,** you hit something hard. *The boy **knocked** on the door with his hand.*

know

(knows, knew, known, knowing)
1. If you **know** somebody, you have met them before. 2. If you **know** something, it is in your mind. *You **know** how old you are.*

Kwanza

Kwanza is an African American holiday that celebrates harvest.

lab

A **lab** is a place for studying and watching experiments.

ladder

A **ladder** is a set of steps that lets you climb up to and down from tall places. *A firefighter uses a **ladder** to reach a high building.*

lady

(ladies)
A **lady** is a woman.

ladybug

A **ladybug** is a small, round insect that flies. A **ladybug** is often red with black spots.

lake

A **lake** is a lot of water with land all around it.

lamb

A **lamb** is a baby sheep. A **lamb** has soft white or black wool.

lamp

A **lamp** lights up a dark place. *A switch turns on the lightbulb in the **lamp**.*

land

(lands, landed, landing)
1. When something **lands,** it comes down from the air onto the ground. *A bird **lands** on the grass.* 2. **Land** is the part of Earth not covered by water.

lap

When you are sitting, your **lap** is the top of your legs. *The pretty lady put a blanket across her **lap**.*

A B C D E F G H I J K L M N O P Q R S T U V W X Y Z

large
(larger, largest)
Someone or something that is **large** is very big. *A dinosaur was a **large** animal.*

last
1. When somebody or something is **last,** it means that person or thing is at the end. *The horse came in **last** in the race.* 2. **Last** means the time before. *The girl went to bed late **last** night.*

late
(later, latest)
If you arrive some place after the time you were supposed to arrive there, you are **late.**

later
If you do something **later,** it will be happening at another time yet to come. *You can eat your lunch **later.***

laugh
(laughs, laughed, laughing)
When you **laugh,** you make sounds that show you think something funny is happening.

laundry
Laundry is the dirty clothes that need to be washed.

lawn
A **lawn** is a grassy area around houses or in a park.

lay
(lays, laid, laying)
1. If you **lay** something some place, you put it down. *The girl **laid** the doll on her bed.* 2. Chickens and birds **lay** eggs.

lead
(leads, led, leading)
1. If you **lead** someone, you go in front to show the way. *The teacher **leads** the children in the line.* 2. **Lead** is a very heavy, gray metal.

leaf
(leaves)
A **leaf** is a thin, flat part that grows on a plant. *Usually, green **leaves** make the food the plant needs.*

leap
(leaps, leaped, leaping)
When you **leap** over something, you take a big jump over it with your feet.

learn

(learns, learned, learning)
When you **learn** about something, you find out things you did not know before. *The boy **learns** the words to sing the song.*

least

The **least** means the smallest amount of something. *Wear the **least** amount of clothes to stay cool in the summer.*

leave

(leaves, left, leaving)
1. When you **leave** a place, you go away from it. *You must **leave** your room to take a bath in the tub.* 2. If you **leave** something somewhere, you go away without it. *You **left** your backpack behind on the school bus.*

leg

Your **leg** is the long part of your body that you stand and walk on.

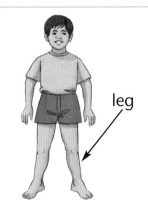

leg

lemon

A **lemon** is a yellow fruit with a thick skin. The juice of the **lemon** tastes sour.

lemonade

Lemonade is a drink people make with lemon juice, sugar, and water. **Lemonade** tastes sweet and sour!

lend

(lends, lent, lending)
If you **lend** someone something, you give it to them to use for a time, and then they give it back to you. *I will **lend** you my sweater until you get warm.*

leopard

A **leopard** is a large wild cat with spots in its fur. A leopard runs very fast.

less

Less means not as much of something. *The boy prefers **less** milk on his cereal than his sister does.*

let

(lets, let, letting)
If someone **lets** you do something, you are allowed to do it. *Your parents **let** you sleep over at your friend's house.*

letter

1. A **letter** is a special mark that you use to write words. *The **letters** C, A, and T spell cat.* 2. A **letter** is a note you write on paper to send to someone.

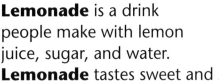

lettuce

Lettuce is a vegetable with big green leaves. Many salads are made with **lettuce** leaves.

library

(libraries)
A **library** is a place where books are kept. People can borrow books from the public **library.**

lick

(licks, licked, licking)
When you **lick** something, you move your tongue across it. *The girl **licked** the ice cream cone.*

lid

A **lid** is the top part of a box, can, or jar. You can open and shut a **lid.**

lie

(lies, lay, lain, lied, lying)
1. When you **lie** somewhere, you rest with your body flat on something. *The baby **lies** down in the crib.* 2. A **lie** is something that is not true. *I **lied** when I said I was as tall as a house!*

life

(lives)
Life is the time when someone or something is alive. *Some people say a cat has nine **lives.***

life preserver

A **life preserver** is a floating device that keeps you from sinking in deep water. Some **life preservers** are rings. You can wear other **life preservers** as vests or belts.

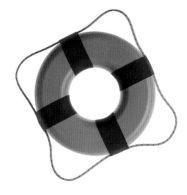

lift

(lifts, lifted, lifting)
If you **lift** something, you pick it up. *You **lift** up your little brother so he can see above the table.*

light

(lights, lit, lighting)
1. When you **light** something, you make it burn. *They **lit** the birthday candles.* 2. **Light** comes from the sun, lamps, and candles and helps you see. 3. If a color is **light,** it is not very dark. *Pink is a **light** color.* 4. If something is **light,** it is not heavy, and it is easy to lift. *A balloon is very **light.***

74

lightbulb

A **lightbulb** is the part of a lamp that makes light. A **lightbulb** is made out of glass with wires inside.

lightning

Lightning is a bright flash of light and electricity you see in the sky when there is a thunderstorm. Sometimes **lightning** hits the ground.

like

(likes, liked, liking)
1. If you **like** something, you enjoy it. *I like eating pizza.* 2. When something is **like** something else, it is similar to it, or a match. *His hat looks like his brother's hat.*

likely

If something is **likely,** it will probably happen. *I see lightning, so it will likely rain.*

lily

(lilies)
A **lily** is a plant that grows from a big bulb in the ground. **Lilies** have beautiful funnel-shape, sweet-smelling flowers.

lime

A **lime** is a sour-tasting, green fruit.

line

1. A long, thin mark is a **line.** *The child drew a line on a paper with his pencil.*
2. When things are in a row, they are in a **line.** *The children walk to the lunchroom in a line.*

lion

A **lion** is a big wild animal in the cat family with light brown fur and a long tail. The male **lion** has thick hair around its head called a mane.

lip

Your two **lips** are around the outside of your mouth. *You make a curve with your lips when you smile.*

list

A **list** has words written down one after the other. *Dad made a grocery list.*

listen
(listens, listened, listening)
When you **listen** to someone, you try to hear what she is saying. *He **listened** on the telephone.*

---

little
(littler, littlest)
When something is **little,** it is small. *A ladybug is a **little** beetle.*

---

live
(lives, lived, living)
1. If someone or something **lives,** that person or thing is alive. *The cat eats mice to **live.*** 2. If you **live** somewhere, that is where your home is. *Grandma and Grandpa **live** by the lake.*

---

living
If someone or something has life, it means that person or thing is **living.** *The baby bunny is breathing, so it is **living.***

---

lizard
A **lizard** is a small, scaly animal with a long body and a long tail. A **lizard** uses its long tongue to catch and eat flies.

---

llama
A **llama** is a large animal with soft wool. Some **llamas** carry things for people in the mountains.

lobster
A **lobster** has a hard shell and two large claws and lives in the ocean. When cooked, **lobsters** turn red.

---

lock
(locks, locked, locking)
1. If you **lock** something, you keep it fastened. 2. A **lock** is something that keeps doors shut. You can open a **lock** with a key.

---

log
A **log** is a long piece of wood cut from the trunk of a tree. Some **logs** are burned in fireplaces.

---

lollipop
A **lollipop** is sweet, colorful candy on a stick that you lick with your tongue.

---

long
(longer, longest)
1. Something that is **long** has a large distance from one end to the other. *A lion has a **long** tail.* 2. **Long** means something lasts for more than a short time. *Night seems to last for a **long** time.*

look
(looks, looked, looking)
You **look** with your eyes to see something.

lose
(loses, lost, losing)
1. If you **lose** something, you cannot find it. *The dog **lost** its bone.* 2. When you **lose** a game, you do not win it. *Dad **lost** the chess game.*

loud
(louder, loudest)
When something is **loud,** it makes a lot of noise. *A drum is a **loud** instrument.*

love
(loves, loved, loving)
If you **love** someone, you like that person very, very much. *I **love** my baby sister and give her lots of hugs.*

lovely
(lovelier, loveliest)
When something is **lovely,** it is very beautiful. *It is a **lovely** sunset.*

low
(lower, lowest)
If something is **low,** it is near the ground. *The baby crawls **low** on the floor.*

luck
Luck is when something good or bad happens by chance. *I hope you have good **luck** winning the door prize.*

lucky
(luckier, luckiest)
If you are **lucky,** something good has happened or will happen to make you happy. *You were very **lucky** to find that five-dollar bill!*

lumber
Wood that is used to build things is called **lumber.**

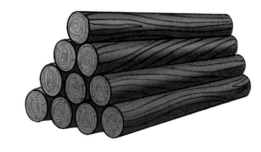

lunch
(lunches)
Lunch is a meal people eat in the middle of the day. *You can carry your **lunch** to school.*

machine

A **machine** is something with parts that move together to do a job, such as a car or bicycle.

mad

(madder, maddest)
When you are **mad,** you are very angry. *I am very **mad** that my friend knocked down my blocks.*

magic

Magic is a special way to do tricks that makes impossible things look real.

magician

A **magician** is a person who does magic tricks. A **magician** may wear a black cape and wave a wand.

magnet

A **magnet** is a piece of metal that other metals stick to. *A **magnet** picks up pins.*

magnifying glass

A **magnifying glass** is a glass lens that makes small things look bigger when you look through it.

mail

The **mail** is letters and packages that you send to or get from other people. *You can get your **mail** at the post office.*

mailbox

(mailboxes)
A **mailbox** holds letters at your house. You can also mail letters by dropping them into a **mailbox** on the street.

make

(makes, made, making)
You can **make** something happen because of something that you do to it. *You can **make** a cake by mixing flour, eggs, and sugar.*

makeup

People put **makeup** on their faces to add color to their lips, cheeks, eyes, and mouth. *Lipstick is a kind of **makeup.***

mall

A **mall** is a place with a lot of stores where people go shopping.

man

(men)
When a boy grows up, he becomes a **man**. *My daddy is a **man.***

mango

(mangoes)
A **mango** is a yellowish-red fruit that tastes sweet and juicy.

many

(more, most)
Many means a large number of something. ***Many** ants came to our picnic.*

map

A **map** is a drawing that shows you where different places are, like towns, rivers, and roads.

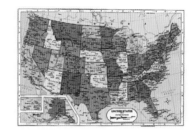

marble

A **marble** is a small glass ball used in games. **Marbles** come in many pretty colors.

march

(marches, marched, marching)
People **march** together by taking the same size steps at the same time. *Soldiers and bands **march** at parades.*

March

March is the third month of the year. *St. Patrick's Day is always **March** 17.*

mark

A **mark** is a spot or line left on something. *When you write, a pencil makes a **mark** on the paper.*

marker

A **marker** is a colored pen that is used for writing or drawing on paper.

A B C D E F G H I J K L M N O P Q R S T U V W X Y Z

marry
(marries, married, marrying)
When a man and a woman **marry,** they become husband and wife.

Mars
Mars, called the red planet, is a little more than half the size of Earth. **Mars** is the fourth planet from the Sun in the solar system.

marshmallow
A **marshmallow** is a soft, white, chewy food. *People roast* **marshmallows** *over campfires.*

mask
A **mask** is something you wear over your face to hide it or protect it. *People wear* **masks** *to look like something else at Halloween.*

mat
A **mat** is a small rug. *We put a welcome* **mat** *near the front door for people to wipe their feet on.*

match
(matches, matched, matching)
1. If things **match,** they are alike in some way. *The brown socks* **match** *the brown shoes.* 2. A **match** is a thin stick you strike to make a fire. 3. A **match** is a game between two players or teams. *The blue team won the soccer* **match.**

math
People learn about numbers when they study **math.** You use your **math** skills when you count and add numbers together.

matter
(matters, mattered, mattering)
If something **matters,** it is important to you. *It really* **matters** *that I learn these spelling words.*

may
1. **May** means that something could happen. *It* **may** *snow today.* 2. **May** means that something is allowed. *Mother says I* **may** *walk to the store.*

May

May is the fifth month of the year. *On **May** Day, children often dance around the maypole.*

maybe

Maybe means perhaps something might happen. ***Maybe** you will be able to go swimming today if it stops raining.*

me

Me means I or myself. *Please give the jump rope to **me**.*

mean

(means, meant, meaning)
1. If you say what something **means,** you explain it. *If we put on our pajamas, this **means** it is almost time for bed.* 2. If you **mean** to do something, you plan to do it. *I **mean** to return your book.* 3. If someone is **mean,** he is not very nice. *That **mean** child hit me.*

meat

Meat is a food that comes from animals. *Beef is the **meat** from a cow.*

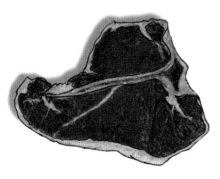

medicine

Medicine is something, like a pill or a shot, that a doctor gives to sick people to make them better.

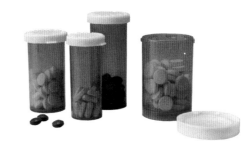

meet

(meets, met, meeting)
When you **meet** somebody, you both get together at the same place at the same time.

melon

A **melon** is a sweet, juicy fruit that grows on a vine. Watermelon is one kind of **melon.**

menorah

A **menorah** is a special candlestick that holds candles to help celebrate the Jewish holiday Hanukkah.

Mercury

Mercury is the smallest planet in the solar system. **Mercury** is the closest planet to the Sun.

A B C D E F G H I J K L M N O P Q R S T U V W X Y Z

mermaid

A **mermaid**, with a female's body and a fish's tail, lives in the ocean in books and movies. **Mermaids** are make-believe.

mess

(messes)

A **mess** is when things are not where they belong. *Your desk is a* **mess** *when your homework is all over it.*

message

A **message** is words that you send or leave when you cannot speak to a person. *Write a* **message** *for the babysitter.*

metal

Metal is something hard that comes out of the ground such as gold, silver, and iron. *Metal is used to make jewelry, cars, and many other machines.*

microphone

You can talk or sing into a **microphone** to make sounds louder.

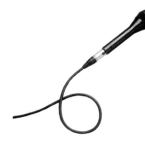

microscope

A **microscope** is an instrument that you look through to make very tiny things appear bigger.

middle

The **middle** is the place that is the same length away from all sides of something. *The bird sits right in the* **middle** *of its cage.*

might

Might means that someone or something could do something. *I* **might** *go to the movies tonight.*

mile

A **mile** is a measurement of 5,280 feet. *It is five* **miles** *down the road to the nearest library.*

milk

Milk is a white liquid that is good for you to drink. Babies drink **milk** from their mother or from cows.

milk shake

A **milk shake** is a sweet drink made by mixing milk and ice cream. *Tasty* **milk shakes** *are made in flavors, such as chocolate and strawberry.*

mind

(minds, minded, minding)
1. If you **mind** something, you are not happy about it. *I **mind** that you are bothering me.* 2. To **mind** means to do what someone, like your parent, tells you to do. 3. Your **mind** is like your brain. You think with your **mind.**

minute

A **minute** is a short amount of time. There are 60 **minutes** in one hour.

mirror

A **mirror** is a special glass that reflects an image. *You look into the **mirror** to see yourself.*

miss

(misses, missed, missing)
1. If you **miss** something, like a ball, you did not hit it or catch it. 2. If you **miss** somebody, you are sad because you aren't with him. *I **miss** my dog who ran away.*

mistake

If you make a **mistake,** you do something wrong. *I left the ice cream out of the freezer and let it melt by **mistake.***

mitten

A **mitten** keeps your hand warm. A **mitten** has one place for your thumb and another space for all your fingers together.

mix

(mixes, mixed, mixing)
You **mix** things together when you stir them up to make something new. *You make a milk shake when you **mix** milk and ice cream.*

mixer

1. A **mixer** is a big truck that mixes cement. The drum on a **mixer** turns and pours the cement inside it to the ground. 2. A **mixer** is a tool used in the kitchen to mix ingredients. *The cook used a **mixer** to mix the pancake batter.*

mobile

A **mobile** is a toy that hangs over a baby's bed. *The **mobile** moves and turns while the baby watches.*

model

A **model** is a small copy of something. *The children built a **model** of a train.*

A B C D E F G H I J K L M N O P Q R S T U V W X Y Z

moment

A **moment** is a short amount of time. *He will be ready to go to school with you in just a **moment**.*

Monday

Monday is the first day of the week after the weekend.

money

You use **money,** like coins and bills, to pay for things you buy.

monkey

A **monkey** is an animal with long arms and legs and a long tail. **Monkeys** are good at climbing trees.

monster

A **monster** is a big scary creature in books and movies.

month

A **month,** like January, is part of the year. There are 12 **months** in a year.

moon

The **moon** is the big bright light that you see in the sky at night. The **moon** travels around Earth about once a month.

mop

A **mop** is a tool with a long handle and a sponge or long stringy head used for cleaning floors. The head of the **mop** is usually dipped in water.

more

More means a bigger amount or size. *His pants have **more** pockets than mine.*

morning

The **morning** is the early part of the day before noon. The sun rises in the **morning.**

most

Most means the biggest number or amount. *I have the **most** popcorn!*

mother

A **mother** is a woman who has a child.

motor

A **motor** is a machine that makes things go. *The **motor** inside of a car makes it run.*

motorcycle

A **motorcycle** is a big bicycle with an engine. One or two people can ride a **motorcycle,** and it can go as fast as a car.

mountain

A **mountain** is a very high hill. The top of a **mountain,** called a peak, sometimes has snow on it.

mouse

(mice)

1. A **mouse** is a small, furry animal with a long, thin tail and sharp teeth. A **mouse** lives in a forest, a field, or a house. 2. A **mouse** is a small piece of equipment you use to move things around a computer screen.

mouth

Your **mouth** is the part of your face that you use to talk and eat. Your **mouth** opens and closes.

mouth

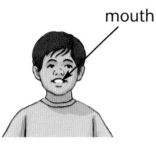

move

(moves, moved, moving)

To **move** means to go from one place to another. *Pick up your lunch and move it to the kitchen.*

mover

A **mover** is someone who brings your things, like furniture, into a new house or an office.

movie

A **movie** is a story told with moving pictures on a big screen or a TV.

much

(more, most)

Much means a big amount. *The horse is eating **much** of the grass in the meadow.*

mud

Mud is soft, wet earth. *The children make **mud** pies after the rain.*

muffin

A **muffin** is a small, sweet cake that people like to eat for breakfast. Some **muffins** have nuts or pieces of fruit inside.

A B C D E F G H I J K L M N O P Q R S T U V W X Y Z

A B C D E F G H I J K L M N O P Q R S T U V W X Y Z

mug

A **mug** is a big cup with a flat bottom and a handle. People drink coffee and hot cocoa from a **mug.**

multiply

(multiplies, multiplied, multiplying)
When you **multiply** a number, you add it to itself a certain number of times. Two multiplied by five is ten: 2×5=10. The sign to **multiply** is ×.

mum

A **mum** is a colorful flower that blooms in the fall of the year. **Mum** is short for chrysanthemum.

muscle

A **muscle** is a body tissue that creates movement. The **muscles** around your mouth make you smile.

mushroom

A mushroom is a type of umbrella-shaped plant that grows in damp, dark places. You can eat some **mushrooms,** but other ones can make you sick.

music

Music is the sound that comes from playing an instrument, like a horn, or from singing with your voice.

must

If you **must** do something, you need to or are commanded to do it. *You **must** breathe to live.*

mustard

Mustard is a thick, spicy, yellow or brownish liquid food that people put on hot dogs or sandwiches.

my

My relates to something that belongs to me or myself. *That is **my** hot dog.*

mystery

(mysteries)
A **mystery** is something odd that happens that cannot be explained. *How the tree fell down is a **mystery.***

nail

1. A **nail** is a short, pointy piece of metal that you hit on its head with a hammer to build something. **Nails** hold things together.

2. Your **nails** are the smooth, shiny, hard ends of your toes and fingers.

name

A **name** is what you call somebody or something.

nap

A **nap** is a short rest. *A puppy takes several naps during the day.*

napkin

A **napkin** is a folded piece of cloth or paper that you use while you eat. People wipe their faces and hands with **napkins.**

nature

Nature is everything on Earth that is not made by people.

near

(nearer, nearest)
If something is **near,** it is not far away. *My neck is near my face.*

nearly

Nearly means almost but not quite. *We are nearly home.*

neat

(neater, neatest)
If you are **neat,** you are not messy. *When you brush your hair, it looks neat.*

neck

Your **neck** joins your shoulders to your head.

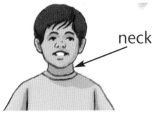

neck

necklace

A **necklace** is something pretty that people wear around their necks. A **necklace** is a string of shiny metal, beads, or jewels.

need

(needs, needed, needing)
If you **need** something, you must have it. *The baby needs her bottle.*

needle

1. A **needle** is a long, thin, sharp piece of metal used for sewing. There is a tiny hole in the top of the **needle** for thread to go through.
2. A **needle** is a thin, sharp, green leaf of a pine tree.

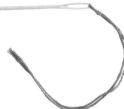

neighbor

A **neighbor** is someone who lives near you.

Neptune

Neptune is the eighth planet from the Sun. **Neptune** is the fourth largest planet in the solar system. Like Earth, **Neptune** orbits around the Sun.

nest

A **nest** is a home that birds and some animals build for their young out of mud, straw, or sticks. Birds lay eggs in **nests.**

net

1. A **net** is pieces of string tied together with holes in between. People catch fish or butterflies in **nets.**
2. A **net** is used with balls in different games, like tennis and soccer. 3. **Net** is another word for the Internet. The **Net** is a system where computers give and receive information.

never

Never means not at any time. *You must **never** play with matches.*

new

(newer, newest)
1. If something is **new,** it has just been made or has not been used. *The girl has **new** shoes.* 2. **New** also means different. *We just moved to a **new** house.*

news

News is information about things that have happened. *Good **news**! My brother is feeling better.*

newspaper

A **newspaper** is many folded sheets of paper with words and pictures on them. You can read about what is happening in the world in the **newspaper.**

next

Next means the one after this one.
Next week is my birthday party.

nice

(nicer, nicest)
If something is **nice,** you feel good about it and like it. *My new haircut is very nice.*

nickel

A **nickel** is a round coin that is worth five cents.

night

Night is the time of day when the sun goes down and it is dark. *People sleep at night.*

nine

Nine is a number that means one more than eight. 8+1=9.

nineteen

Nineteen is a number that is one more than eighteen. 18+1=19.

ninety

Ninety is a number ten less than one hundred.
Ninety is nine sets of ten.
10+10+10+10+10+10+10+10+10=90.

no

1. **No** means not any. *There are **no** more peanuts left.* 2. **No** means not so. *No, I did not break the glass.* 3. **No** means that you do not have permission. *No, you cannot have some candy.*

nobody

Nobody means no one. *Nobody wanted to eat spinach for dinner.*

nod

(nods, nodded, nodding)
When you **nod** your head, it moves up and down. You can **nod** your head to mean yes.

noise

A **noise** is a sound that someone or something makes. *The dog's bark is a loud noise.*

none

None means not any. *After we ate all the bananas, there were **none** left.*

A B C D E F G H I J K L M N O P Q R S T U V W X Y Z

north

North is a direction. The needle points to **north** on the compass.

nose

Your **nose** is a part of your face that helps you to smell and breathe.

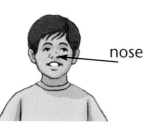

nose

not

Not makes something negative. *My aunt is **not** happy about her missing necklace.*

notebook

A **notebook** has pages for you to write or draw on.

nothing

Nothing means not at all or of no importance. *Your spilled water is **nothing**. We will clean it up.*

November

November is a month in the fall of the year. *Thanksgiving is a holiday in **November**.*

now

Now means at this time. *You are wearing your glasses **now**.*

number

A **number** is a word or sign that says how many things you have. *The symbol 5 means the **number** five.*

nurse

A **nurse** is someone who takes care of sick or hurt people. **Nurses** work in hospitals and doctors' offices.

nut

A **nut** is a seed or fruit that has a hard shell. People crack the shell and eat **nuts** such as cashews and almonds.

oar

An **oar** is a long piece of wood with one flat end. You push the **oar** to row a boat through the water.

oboe

An **oboe** is a long, thin musical instrument. You blow into the **oboe** to make sounds.

ocean

An **ocean** is a very big sea. The water in the **ocean** tastes salty.

October

October is a fall month of the year. *Halloween is a holiday in **October**.*

octopus
(octopuses)
An **octopus** is a sea animal with eight long arms.

off

1. **Off** means away from something. *The ball fell **off** the shelf.* 2. **Off** is the opposite of on. *My brother turned the television **off** so we could eat dinner.*

office

An **office** is a place where people work. An **office** has a desk, a chair, and maybe a computer.

officer

An **officer** is an important person who is in charge of other people. A police **officer** and an army **officer** make sure people follow the rules.

often

If you do something **often,** you do it a lot of times. *We **often** go to the fast-food restaurant to eat.*

oil

Oil is a thick, slippery liquid. Light **oil** that comes from plants is used for cooking. Dark **oil** that comes from the ground helps heat your home and make your car run.

A B C D E F G H I J K L M N O P Q R S T U V W X Y Z

OK

OK, or **okay,** means that things are all right. *It's **OK** that you go to play at your friend's house.*

old

(older, oldest)
1. If someone or something is **old,** they have lived or been around for a long time. *My grandpa is **old** at 90. 2. **Old** means something that you had before. *That looks like my **old** shirt.*

olive

An **olive** is a green or brown vegetable that grows on trees. People eat **olives** in salad and on pizza.

on

1. **On** means atop something. *The bowl is **on** the table. 2. **On** is the opposite of off. *Turn the light **on** so we can see.*

once

1. **Once** means only one time. *We went to the zoo **once**. 2. **Once** means as soon as or after. *You can watch TV **once** you have finished picking up all your toys.*

one

One is a number. **One** comes before two.

onion

An **onion** is a round vegetable with a papery skin. An **onion** has a strong taste and smell.

only

Only means a limited amount. *You can **only** have one piece of watermelon.*

open

(opens, opened, opening)
1. If you take a lid off something, you **open** it. 2. If something is **open,** you can go through it. *They walked through the **open** door.*

or

Or means there is a choice of some kind. *You can pick apples **or** oranges.*

orange

1. **Orange** is a bright color. A pumpkin is **orange.** 2. An **orange** is a sweet, round fruit with an **orange**-colored skin. People squeeze **oranges** to get juice.

organ

1. An **organ** is a musical keyboard instrument like a piano. The music from an **organ** comes out of long pipes. 2. An **organ** is a part of your body that helps you to live, such as your lungs in your chest.

ornament

An **ornament** is a special decoration to make things look pretty. *You can put a Christmas ornament on a tree.*

other

Other means different than the one you have. *Where is your other pencil?*

our

Our means it has to do with or belongs to us. *It is our picnic basket.*

out

1. **Out** means away from the inside. *The cat climbed out of the box.* 2. **Out** means to get rid of. *The forest ranger has put out the campfire.*

outside

Outside means not in something. *The pear is outside the box.*

oven

An **oven** is the hot inside part of the stove where you cook food. **Ovens** have doors that close to keep the heat inside.

over

1. **Over** means across something. *The turtle crawled over the path.* 2. If someone tells you something **over,** they tell it to you again. *Why must I tell you over and over to wear your mittens outside?* 3. **Over** means that something is finished. *When one team wins, the football game is over.*

owl

An **owl** is a bird with large, round eyes that are good for seeing small animals at night. An **owl** makes a hooting sound.

own

(owns, owned, owning)
If you **own** something, it belongs to you. *I own the lion mask.*

A B C D E F G H I J K L M N O P Q R S T U V W X Y Z

pacifier

A **pacifier** has a little rubber end for a baby to suck on. A **pacifier** comforts a crying baby.

package

A **package** holds things. A **package** could be a box or a large envelope that is tied or taped shut.

pad

1. A **pad** is a number of blank pieces of paper on which to write or draw. 2. A **pad** is a soft, thick piece of material that provides comfort. *The babysitter put down a **pad** so he could lay the baby on it.*

page

A **page** is a piece of paper inside a book.

pail

A **pail** is a container used to carry things like water from place to place. A **pail** has a handle and a flat bottom.

paint

(paints, painted, painting)
1. You can use brushes and paints to **paint** or make a colorful picture.
2. When you **paint** a wall or house, you put **paint** on it. 3. **Paint** is a liquid that you can use to put color in pictures or on houses.

paintbrush

(paintbrushes)
A **paintbrush** has a long handle on one end and a group of hairs called bristles on the other. You dip the **paintbrush** in paint and move it back and forth on a surface to spread the paint.

painting

A **painting** is a picture that someone has painted with a brush.

pair

A **pair** is the name for two things that go together. *I have a **pair** of new shoes.*

pajamas

Pajamas are a loose shirt and pants that you wear to bed to sleep in and keep warm.

pal

If someone is your **pal**, that person is a close friend.

palace

A **palace** is a large, special house where a king and queen and their family live.

palm tree

Most **palm trees** have a tall, straight trunk. A **palm tree** has branches with green, feathery leaves on its top. **Palm trees** grow in warm places.

pan

A **pan** is a metal dish with a handle. You cook food in a **pan.** *My brother cooked eggs in a frying **pan** on top of the stove.*

pancake

A **pancake** is a thin, round cake made with flour, eggs, and milk. After you cook the **pancake,** you put butter and syrup on top and then eat it.

panda

A **panda** is a huge black-and-white, furry animal that looks like a bear. **Pandas** live in China.

pants

Pants are clothes that cover the bottom half of your body. **Pants** have two legs and, sometimes, pockets.

papaya

A **papaya** is a fruit with a sweet, yellow inside and yellow, pink, or orange skin. **Papayas** grow on trees in places with warm weather.

paper

Paper is a thin sheet made from cloth or wood. People write and draw on **paper** and wrap things in it, too.

paper clip

A **paper clip** is a curved piece of metal that holds pieces of paper together. *Can you slide the **paper clip** over two pieces of paper?*

park

(parks, parked, parking)
1. When you **park** a car, you leave it somewhere for a while. 2. A **park** is a large grassy place where people can walk and play games.

part

1. A **part** is a piece of something. *A puzzle has lots of different **parts.*** 2. A **part** is a role in a play or show. *You may have a **part** in the school play.*

A B C D E F G H I J K L M N O P Q R S T U V W X Y Z

party
(parties)
When a group of friends get together to eat and have fun, they have a **party.** *You eat cake at a birthday **party.***

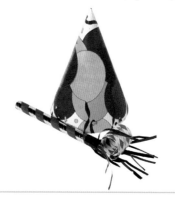

pass
(passes, passed, passing)
1. If you **pass** someone or something, you go by them. *I **passed** the store on the way home.* 2. When you **pass** something to someone, you give it to them. *Can you **pass** me the cookies?*

past
The **past** is the time before now. *In the **past**, there was no TV.*

paste
Paste is white sticky stuff that is used to hold papers together. *Use **paste** to keep your photos in the book.*

pat
(pats, patted, patting)
When you **pat** something, you tap it gently with your fingers or hand.

path
A **path** is a narrow piece of land for people to walk, run, or ride on. *I can ride my bike on the **path** along the river.*

paw
Some animals, such as dogs, have **paws** for feet. A **paw** has claws that help the animals climb, fight, and catch food.

pay
(pays, paid, paying)
When you **pay** someone, you give that person money for something. *He **paid** the lady for the papaya.*

pea
A **pea** is a small, round, green vegetable that grows inside a long pod.

peace
Peace is a quiet time without any fighting between people.

peach
(peaches)
A **peach** is a soft, juicy fruit with a pit inside and yellow-red, fuzzy skin outside.

peacock

A **peacock** is a male bird with beautiful, long, blue and green feathers that fan out in his tail.

peanut

A **peanut** is a seed from a plant. **Peanuts** become ripe under the ground. The small oval **peanuts** found inside a brown shell are roasted before you eat them. Although some people  believe **peanuts** are nuts, they are really more like beans or peas.

peanut butter

Peanut butter is a soft food made from peanuts. You spread sticky **peanut butter** on sandwiches and crackers.

pear

A **pear** is a yellow, green, or brown fruit that is sweet and juicy. One end of the round **pear** is bigger than the other.

pecan

A **pecan** is a nut with a smooth shell that grows on trees. People enjoy eating **pecan** pie.

peel

(peels, peeled, peeling)
1. When you **peel** something, you take the skin off. *Dad used a knife to **peel** an apple for me.* 2. A **peel** is the skin on some fruits and vegetables. *Bananas, oranges, and potatoes have **peels.***

pelican

A **pelican** is a large ocean bird with a huge bill. **Pelicans** use their bills to store fish they catch.

pen

A **pen** is a long, thin tool filled with ink for writing or drawing.

pencil

A **pencil** is a long, thin stick with graphite in the middle. The dark point of a **pencil** makes marks when drawing or writing.

pencil case

A **pencil case** is a special bag or box to hold pencils. *My **pencil case** keeps my pencils from breaking.*

A B C D E F G H I J K L M N O P Q R S T U V W X Y Z

A B C D E F G H I J K L M N O P Q R S T U V W X Y Z

penguin

A **penguin** is a large black-and-white bird that swims in the sea but does not fly. **Penguins** live where it is very cold.

penny
(pennies)

A **penny,** or one cent, is a coin. A **penny** is the smallest amount of money in the United States and Canada.

pepper

1. **Pepper** is a black spicy powder to put on food.
2. A **pepper** is a bright green, yellow, or red vegetable. *I like peppers on my pizza.*

person
(people)

A **person** is a man, a woman, or a child.

pet

A **pet** is an animal, like a dog or cat, that you take care of in your home. People usually give their **pets** names.

petal

A **petal** is a soft, thin, colorful part of a flower. *How many petals does a daisy have?*

phone

Phone is short for *telephone*. A **phone** is a machine that lets you talk and listen to others. Part of the **phone** has numbers for you to push or dial to reach someone.

photograph

A **photograph** is a picture you take with a camera. A **photograph** might be printed in black and white or in color.

piano

A **piano** is a large musical instrument with black keys and white keys that you tap with your fingers to make sounds.

pick
(picks, picked, picking)

1. When you **pick** something, you choose it. *You pick the pizza topping.* 2. If you **pick** some fruit, you take it from the tree. 3. When you **pick** up something, you lift it. *Pick your foot up high.*

pickle

A **pickle** is a cucumber that has soaked in a spicy liquid. **Pickles** you eat come in slices and sticks and can taste sweet or sour.

picnic

A **picnic** is a meal you eat outside. Sandwiches, fruit, and cookies are good **picnic** foods.

picnic basket

A **picnic basket** is a large container with a big handle to carry the picnic food outside.

picture

A **picture** is a painting, drawing, or photograph. **Pictures** can be of animals, plants, or designs.

pie

A **pie** has a crispy crust over a thick filling of fruit, meat, or vegetables. A **pie** is baked in the oven.

piece

A **piece** is a part of something. *I can cut a **piece** of apple pie.*

pig

A **pig** is a fat farm animal with short legs and a curly tail. A **pig** squeals, *oink, oink!*

pigeon

A **pigeon** is a bird whose small head bobs up and down when it walks. **Pigeons** like to sit on statues and rooftops.

piglet

A **piglet** is a baby pig with pink skin. **Piglets** sleep together next to their mother.

pile

A **pile** is a lot of things put one on top of the other. *Look at the big **pile** of laundry.*

pill

A **pill** is a small round piece of medicine that you take to feel better.

pillow

A **pillow** is a bag filled with soft material, like feathers. You rest your head on a **pillow** to go to sleep in bed.

pilot

A **pilot** is someone who flies an airplane. A **pilot** sits in the front of the plane with the controls.

A B C D E F G H I J K L M N O P Q R S T U V W X Y Z

pin

A **pin** is a small, thin metal tool with a sharp pointed end. **Pins** hold pieces of cloth together when you sew.

piñata

A **piñata** is a decorated hollow Mexican toy filled with candy and gifts. Children try to break a hanging **piñata** with a stick so the treats will fall out.

pine

A **pine** tree has needles for leaves that are green all year long. A **pine** tree has long brown pinecones with seeds inside. *A Christmas tree is often **pine**.*

pineapple

A **pineapple** is a yellow-brown fruit with sharp, pointed green leaves on the top. The inside of the **pineapple** is yellow, very juicy, and sweet.

pinecone

Sometimes scaly and sticky, a **pinecone** is something that grows on evergreen trees. **Pinecone** seeds grow into new trees.

pink

When you mix white and red together, you make the color **pink**. *Baby pigs are **pink**.*

pipe

A **pipe** is a long, thin metal or plastic tube. Things like oil and water move through **pipes.**

piranha

A **piranha** is a fish in South America with very sharp teeth. **Piranhas** swim in groups to find a meal.

pirate

A **pirate** is a person who robs ships at sea. **Pirates** are sometimes pictured with eye patches and wooden legs.

pistachio

A **pistachio** is a small round nut with a hard white shell. People roast the little green **pistachio** nut to eat.

pitcher

A **pitcher** is like a big cup with a handle used to store a lot of liquid. You can pour juice or milk from a special opening at the top of a **pitcher.**

pizza

A **pizza** is a flat, round food baked in a very hot oven. You can add tomato sauce, cheese, and other toppings to the **pizza** crust.

place

A **place** is a space or location, like a town or a farm. *Your bedroom is a good place to sleep.*

plain

(plainer, plainest)
1. Something that is **plain** is all one color and does not have a design on it. *You are sitting on a plain chair.* 2. A **plain** is a large area of flat land. *The middle of the United States is made up of the Great Plains.*

plan

(plans, planned, planning)
1. If you **plan** something, you decide how to do it. *We are planning to go on a picnic.* 2. A **plan** is a map of a building. *I am looking at a floor plan of your house.*

plane

A **plane** is a big machine that flies. **Plane** is short for *airplane.*

planet

A **planet** is a huge, round thing in space. Nine **planets,** such as Earth, go around the Sun.

plant

A **plant** is a living thing that grows in dirt or water. Most **plants,** like trees and flowers, have roots, stems, leaves, flowers, and seeds.

plate

A **plate** is a round, flat object that you put food on. *You put cake on a dessert plate.*

play

(plays, played, playing)
1. When you **play,** you have fun. *I play catch with my friend.* 2. If you **play** a musical instrument, you make sounds with it. *My fingers play the piano.* 3. A **play** is a story you act out or watch. *I am Snow White in the school play.*

playground

A **playground** is a place outdoors where you can have fun. *I like to swing on the swings at the playground.*

playpen

A **playpen** is a safe place with four soft sides and a floor for babies to play. Most **playpens** fold up.

please

Please is a word you use when you ask for something in a nice way. *Would you **please** make me a sandwich?*

plenty

If there is **plenty** of something, there is more than you need. *There are **plenty** of carrots for the bunny.*

pliers

A **pliers** is a tool with two moving parts joined near one end. You pinch the tops of a **pliers** together to hold things.

plum

A **plum** is a juicy fruit with smooth green, purple, red, or yellow skin. A **plum** is soft and yellow inside with a big pit.

plumber

A **plumber** is a person who works on water pipes and water machines. A **plumber** fixes a leak in your sink.

plus

You use the word **plus** when you add numbers together. The sign for **plus** is +. *One **plus** three equals four: 1+3=4.*

Pluto

Pluto is the planet in the solar system that is the farthest away from the Sun.

pocket

A **pocket** is a small bag that holds things. **Pockets** are sewn into your clothes so you can keep keys, money, or your hands inside of them.

point

(points, pointed, pointing)
1. When you **point** with your finger, you show where something is located.
2. A **point** is a sharp end of something, such as a pin or a pencil.
3. A **point** is a score in a game. *Your team scored five **points**.*

police

Police are people whose job it is to keep others safe and stop them from breaking the laws. Many **police** officers wear special badges and uniforms.

police car

A **police car** has special flashing lights and a siren that the police turn on if they are chasing people who broke the law. **Police cars** are usually painted special colors and have signs on them.

pom-pom

A **pom-pom** is a fluffy ball made of strings that wiggle when you shake them. *Cheerleaders shake **pom-poms** at football games.*

pond

A **pond** is a small area of water with land around it. *The cow drinks water from the **pond**.*

pony

(ponies)
A **pony** is a small horse that children like to ride. **Ponies** can pull carts.

pool

A **pool** is a place where you can swim in the water.

poor

(poorer, poorest)
Someone who is **poor** does not have a lot of money. *The man cannot afford to buy shoes because he is **poor**.*

pop

(pops, popped, popping)
A **pop** means something burst and made a sharp sound. *If you poke a balloon with a pin, it will **pop**!*

popcorn

Hard **popcorn** seeds burst open and puff out when you heat them. Cooked **popcorn** is white, fluffy, crunchy, and good to eat for a snack!

porcupine

A **porcupine** is an animal with stiff pointed hairs, called quills, on its back. A **porcupine** sticks its quills into an animal that gets too close.

porpoise

A **porpoise** is an underwater animal (but not a fish) with a short nose. A **porpoise** swims very fast in the ocean.

possible

If something is **possible,** it can be done. *If I hold your hand, it is **possible** for me to stand on one foot.*

post

A **post** is a strong pole that stands up in the ground. *The gate is held by the **post**.*

post office

A **post office** is a building where you can send and pick up letters and packages. You can buy stamps and envelopes at the **post office.**

pot

A **pot** is a deep, round pan used for cooking things like soup. A **pot** has one or two handles and a lid.

potato

(potatoes)
A **potato** is a round vegetable that grows underground with brown or red skin. You can boil, fry, mash, and bake **potatoes.**

pour

(pours, poured, pouring)
When you **pour** something, it flows out of the container. *The child **pours** the water from the pitcher.*

power

Power is something strong that makes things happen. ***Power** from the wind makes the windmill turn.*

practice

(practices, practiced, practicing)
When you **practice** something, you do it many times to get better at it. *You **practice** the piano to get ready to play at the show.*

prepare

(prepares, prepared, preparing)
When you **prepare** something, you get it ready. *You can **prepare** scrambled eggs for our breakfast.*

present

1. A **present** is something you give someone for a special reason. *I gave my friend a birthday **present**.*
2. The **present** time is now. *At **present**, all of the ducks are quacking.*

president

A **president** is an important person who others have picked to lead a country or organization.

press

(presses, pressed, pressing)
When you **press** something, you push on it. *You **press** the letters on your computer keyboard.*

104

pretend
(pretends, pretended, pretending)
If you **pretend,** you act as if something that is not true is real. *I am **pretending** to be a scary monster.*

pretty
(prettier, prettiest)
When someone or something is **pretty,** that person or thing is very nice to look at. *The rainbow is very **pretty.***

pretzel
A **pretzel** is a snack food baked in different shapes like sticks or knots. **Pretzels** are crunchy and salty.

price
The **price** is how much money something costs. *The **price** of the coat is on the tag.*

prince
A **prince** is the son of the king or queen. A **prince** lives in a palace.

princess
(princesses)
A **princess** is the daughter of the king or queen. A **princess** lives in a palace.

print
(prints, printed, printing)
When people **print** words and pictures, they put them on paper with a pencil, a pen, or a machine.

printer
A **printer** is a machine that makes marks on paper. A computer tells the **printer** what kinds of marks to make.

prize
A **prize** is something you win when you do well. A **prize** might be a ribbon, a trophy, or money.

problem
1. A **problem** is something difficult to understand. *It is a **problem** for me to put this puzzle together.* 2. A **problem** is when something is wrong. *It is a **problem** when the children don't listen to the teacher.*

promise
(promises, promised, promising)
If you **promise,** you say that you will really do something. *I **promise** to take my little brother to the playground.*

A B C D E F G H I J K L M N O P Q R S T U V W X Y Z

puck

A **puck** is a hard, round rubber disc used to play ice hockey. Players hit the **puck** with long sticks, and it slides across the ice.

pull

(pulls, pulled, pulling)
When you move someone or something toward you, you **pull** it. *You **pull** on the oar to row the boat.*

pump

A **pump** is a tool that gases and liquids pass through. A **pump** can put air into a flat bicycle tire.

pumpkin

A **pumpkin** is a large, round orange fruit that you can cook and make into **pumpkin** pies. *People carve faces in **pumpkins** for Halloween.*

puppet

A **puppet** is a doll you make move. Some **puppets** move when you put your hand inside them, while others move when you pull strings.

puppy

(puppies)
A **puppy** is a young dog. **Puppies** like to play and chew on things.

purple

When you mix red and blue, you make the color **purple**. *A plum is **purple**.*

purpose

When you have a **purpose** for doing something, you have a plan. *My **purpose** for getting out the paper, scissors, and paste is to make valentines.*

purse

A **purse** is a bag with a handle or strap that people carry things in such as money and keys.

push

(pushes, pushed, pushing)
When you move someone or something away from you, you **push** it.

put

(puts, put, putting)
If you **put** something somewhere, you move it there. *I **put** my foot on the floor.*

puzzle

A **puzzle** is a game, toy, or question that you have fun trying to figure out. *How do I put this **puzzle** together?*

quart

A **quart** is a measure for liquids, such as milk. There are four **quarts** in a gallon.

quarter

1. A **quarter** is one of four equal parts of something. *You can have a quarter of the pizza.*
2. A **quarter** is a silver coin. One **quarter** is the same value as 25 pennies.

queen

A **queen** is a woman who rules a country. A **queen** is sometimes married to a king.

question

You ask a **question** when you want to find out about something. *My teacher had a good answer to my question.*

quick

(quicker, quickest)
1. If someone moves fast, he is **quick.**
2. **Quick** also means something must be done in a short time.

quiet

(quieter, quietest)
If someone is **quiet,** she doesn't make any noise. *Be quiet in the library.*

quilt

A **quilt** is two pieces of cloth stuffed with soft material and sewn together. People sew pretty designs on **quilts** and use them for a warm bed cover.

quit

(quits, quit, quitting)
If you **quit** something, you stop doing it. *I quit playing soccer because I broke my foot when I fell.*

quiz

(quizzes)
A **quiz** is a short test that asks questions to find out how much you know. *My teacher gave me a quiz to see if I could spell animal names.*

rabbit

A **rabbit** is a small, wild, furry animal with long ears. A **rabbit** moves by hopping. **Rabbits** like to eat carrots.

raccoon

A **raccoon** is a furry animal with a long, ringed tail and a black fur mask around its eyes. A **raccoon** sleeps in the day and looks for food at night.

race

To find out who or what can go the fastest, people have a contest called a **race.** *The woman with blue shorts won the **race** around the block.*

rack

A **rack** is a frame to display or store things in. *I can hang my hat on the **rack.***

radio

A **radio** is a machine that picks up waves in the air and turns them into sounds.

radish

(radishes)
A **radish** is a spicy red-and-white vegetable that grows under the ground. You might eat **radishes** in a salad.

railroad

A **railroad** is a path made of metal bars for a train's wheels to follow. *Railroad tracks go across bridges and mountains.*

rain

Rain is small drops of water that fall to the ground from clouds in the sky.

rainbow

A **rainbow** is a curved band of colors you sometimes see in the sky when the sun shines after the rain.

raincoat

You wear a **raincoat** to keep yourself dry from the rain.

raisin

A **raisin** is a small dried grape. Chewy and sweet, **raisins** are good in cereal or for a snack.

rake

A **rake** is a tool with a long handle and big teeth that you use to collect leaves and grass outdoors.

Ramadan

Ramadan is the ninth month of the Islamic year. During **Ramadan,** people do not eat between dawn and sunset.

raspberry

(raspberries)
A **raspberry** is a small, bumpy, black or red fruit with many tiny seeds. **Raspberries** grow on bushes.

rat

A **rat** is an animal that looks like a big mouse with a long, thin tail and very sharp teeth. A **rat** makes a *squeak, squeak* sound.

rattle

When you shake a **rattle,** the loose parts inside make sharp, short sounds. A **rattle** is a baby's toy.

rattlesnake

A **rattlesnake** is a very long animal that has scales and moves by wiggling. The **rattlesnake** warns people it might hurt them by making a rattling noise with its tail.

raw

(rawer, rawest)
If a food is **raw,** it is not cooked. *Raw carrots crunch when you eat them.*

ray

A **ray** is a thin beam of light. *A ray from the flashlight shines through the night.*

reach

(reaches, reached, reaching)
When you **reach** for something, you put your hand out for it. *You reach to pick the flower.* 2. When you **reach** a place, you arrive there. *It will be time to swim when we reach the pond.*

read

(reads, read, reading)
When you **read,** you look at words and know what they mean.

ready

(readier, readiest)

If you are **ready,** you are prepared to do something right now. *As soon as you are **ready,** we will go to the store.*

real

If something is **real,** it is true. *Is this a **real** story or a make-believe one?*

reason

A **reason** explains why something happens. *The **reason** you are wet is because you did not wear your raincoat in the rain.*

rectangle

A **rectangle** is a shape with two long sides, two short sides, and four corners. *A door is a **rectangle**.*

red

Red is a color. *Fire engines and cherries are **red** things.*

referee

A **referee** is a person who makes sure the players follow the rules at games such as football and basketball.

refrigerator

A **refrigerator** is a machine that keeps food cold and fresh. The coldest part of the **refrigerator** is the freezer.

remember

(remembers, remembered, remembering)

If you **remember** something, you keep it in your mind. *I **remembered** to get the cake out of the oven.*

rent

(rents, rented, renting)

If you **rent** something, you pay someone money to use it for a while. *My parents **rent** the house we live in.*

reply

(replies, replied, replying)

When you **reply,** you give someone an answer. *I am **replying** to your phone call.*

report

When you write or give a **report,** you tell about something. *I wrote a **report** for my teacher about growing seeds.*

reptile

A **reptile** is an animal that has cold blood and skin with scales on it. **Reptiles,** such as snakes and turtles, lay eggs.

rescue

(rescues, rescued, rescuing)
If you **rescue** somebody, you help them or save them from danger. *The firefighter **rescued** the cat from the tree.*

rest

(rests, rested, resting)
1. When you **rest,** you stop what you are doing because you are tired. *After playing in the park, you need to **rest.***
2. The **rest** is what is left over when a part of something has been taken away. *I will give you the **rest** of the cake.*

return

(returns, returned, returning)
When you **return** something, you give it back. *I am **returning** your hockey puck because I'm finished playing.*

ribbon

A **ribbon** is a long, thin piece of colored cloth or paper used to decorate gifts or someone's hair. **Ribbons** are also sometimes given out for a prize. *If someone wins first place, they get a blue **ribbon.***

rice

Rice is a small white or brown seed that gets soft when you cook it for food. **Rice** grows in wet land in hot countries.

rich

(richer, richest)
If someone is **rich,** that person has a lot of money or things, like jewelry. *The **rich** man owns five cars.*

riddle

A **riddle** is a puzzling question that has a funny answer. *A **riddle:** What is black and white and read all over? (A newspaper!)*

ride

(rides, rode, ridden, riding)
To **ride** is to travel in or on something. People may **ride** bikes, horses, buses, or other moving things.

right

1. If something is **right,** it is not wrong. *All the answers on my quiz were **right.***
2. **Right** is the opposite of left. *I roll the bowling ball with my **right** hand.*

ring
(rings, rang, rung, ringing)
1. If something **rings,** it sounds like a bell. 2. A **ring** is a piece of pretty jewelry you wear on your finger. 3. A **ring** is a circle shape with an empty center. *The children held hands and made a* ***ring*** *to play the game.*

rip
(rips, ripped, ripping)
When you tear or cut something open, you **rip** it. *I **ripped** open the envelope to pull out the letter.*

rise
(rises, rose, risen, rising)
If something **rises,** it moves up. *The sun **rises** every morning.*

river
A **river** is a long, wide bit of water with land on both sides. A **river** flows to the sea.

road
A **road** is a wide path that cars, buses, and trucks use to travel between places. Most **roads** are hard and smooth.

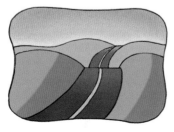

roar
(roars, roared, roaring)
1. To **roar** is to make a loud, low sound. *The lion **roared** when it was angry.* 2. A long, very loud sound is a **roar.** *We could not hear the pilot over the **roar** of the airplane.*

rob
(robs, robbed, robbing)
If people **rob** someone, they take things that do not belong to them. *The people who **robbed** the bank took a lot of money.*

robin
A **robin** is a songbird with red feathers on its breast.

robot
A **robot** is a machine that does some work that people do. Computerized **robots** can build cars in factories.

rock
(rocks, rocked, rocking)
1. When you **rock** something, you move it back and forth or side to side. *Mommy **rocks** the baby in the **rocking** chair.* 2. A **rock** is a hard stone that comes from the earth. **Rock** rises from the earth as mountains.

rocket

A **rocket** is a tubelike machine that flies very fast and very high. Burning gasses inside the **rocket** make it shoot into space.

rocking chair

A **rocking chair** is a seat with two curved rockers on the bottom that help it move back and forth. *Babies like to be rocked to sleep in a **rocking chair**.*

roll

(rolls, rolled, rolling)
1. When something round, like a ball, **rolls,** it moves by turning over and over. 2. A **roll** is a little round piece of baked bread. *People make sandwiches with **rolls**.*

roof

A **roof** is the flat or pointed top part of a building that covers it to keep out the rain. Cars and trucks also have a flat **roof** on the top.

room

1. A **room** is a space with walls around it inside a building. *A kitchen is a **room**.* 2. **Room** also means space. *Is there **room** for me in the bed?*

rooster

A **rooster**, a male chicken with a fancy tail, lives on a farm. A **rooster** makes a noisy *cock-a-doodle-do* sound.

rope

A **rope** is a thick, strong set of strings twisted together. You can use **rope** to lift, pull, or tie things.

rose

A **rose** is a sweet-smelling, beautiful flower with sharp points called thorns on its stem. **Roses** grow on bushes.

rough

(rougher, roughest)
Something that is **rough** is not smooth. Sandpaper is **rough**.

round

(rounder, roundest)
Something that is **round** has the same shape as a circle or a ball.

row

(rows, rowed, rowing)
1. When you **row** a boat, you move it through the water with oars. 2. A **row** is a line of people or things. *The girl put her teddy bears in a **row.***

rowboat

A **rowboat** is something that people sit in to ride through the water. They use two oars to move the **rowboat** along.

rub

(rubs, rubbed, rubbing)
When you **rub** a thing, you move your hand back and forth across it. *When you **rub** your kitty, it purrs.*

rubber

Rubber is a material that stretches and bounces. *The **rubber** playground ball bounces high.*

rubber band

A **rubber band** is a long circle of stretchy rubber that can slide over things to hold them in place.

rug

A **rug** is a strong, sturdy cloth used to cover a floor.

rule

(rules, ruled, ruling)
1. If someone **rules** a country, they control the people who live there. 2. A **rule** lets you know what you can do. *A classroom **rule** says to throw away your juice cups after snack time.*

ruler

1. A **ruler** is a tool that helps you measure how long something is or draw a straight line. 2. A **ruler** is a person who is the leader of the country.

run

(runs, ran, running)
When you **run,** you move your legs very quickly. If you **run,** you go faster than walking.

sad
(sadder, saddest)
If you are **sad,** you feel unhappy. *You are **sad** that you broke your arm.*

safe
(safer, safest)
If you are **safe,** nothing can hurt you, and you are not in danger. *I am **safe** in the water wearing my life jacket.*

sailor
A **sailor** is someone who works on a ship. **Sailors** keep ships clean and running smoothly.

salad
A **salad** is a cold mixture of fruits, vegetables, or meats. You might eat dressing on top of a **salad.**

salt
Salt is a white powder people put on food for flavor. *Pretzels have **salt** on them.*

same
If two things are the **same,** they are just like each other. *The girls' hair ribbons are blue and look the **same.***

sandwich
(sandwiches)
A **sandwich** is two slices of bread with food, such as meat, cheese, and vegetables, in between.

Santa Claus
Santa Claus is a jolly old man with a round belly who leaves gifts for children on Christmas Eve. **Santa Claus** dresses in a red suit and rides in a sleigh pulled by flying reindeer.

Saturday
Saturday is the seventh day of the week. You do not go to school on **Saturday,** a weekend day.

Saturn

Saturn is a planet in the solar system that is larger than Earth. **Saturn** has rings around it.

sausage

Sausage is spicy chopped meat stuffed into a long skin and then cooked.

save

(saves, saved, saving)
1. If you **save** money or anything else, you keep it some place to use later on. *I'm **saving** pennies in my piggy bank.*
2. If you **save** someone, you rescue her from danger. *The firefighter **saved** the kitten that was stuck in the tree.*

saxophone

A **saxophone** is a musical instrument that sounds like a horn. You blow into a **saxophone** and press the keys to change the sounds.

say

(says, said, saying)
When you **say** something, you speak words with your mouth. *The girl **says** she likes cheese.*

scare

(scares, scared, scaring)
If something **scares** you, you feel afraid. *All the thunder and lightning **scared** the dog.*

scarecrow

A **scarecrow** looks like a huge doll dressed in old clothes. Stuffed with straw, a **scarecrow** frightens birds away from a farmer's field.

scarf

(scarves)
A **scarf** is a long piece of material you wear around your head or neck to keep warm.

school

School is a place where people go to learn. In **school**, the teacher helps children learn to read, write, and do math.

science

Science is the study of things like animals, plants, and the planets.

scientist

A **scientist** is a person who studies about the world and how it works. A **scientist** might study about one thing, such as the stars.

scissors

A pair of **scissors** is a cutting tool with two sharp, pointed parts joined together. **Scissors** can cut cloth or paper.

score

When you play a game, the **score** tells how many points each team has. *The score of the baseball game is 7–5.*

scream

(screams, screamed, screaming)
If you **scream,** you yell.

screen

1. A **screen** is a big, flat area where you see a TV or a movie picture. 2. A **screen** looks like a metal or plastic net with tiny holes to fit over a window or door. A **screen** keeps the bugs out.

sea

A **sea** is a large body of salty water.

sea horse

A **sea horse** is a small ocean fish that swims by waving a fin on its back. The top part of the **sea horse** looks like a horse, while the bottom part has a curly tail.

seal

(seals, sealed, sealing)
1. If you **seal** something, you close it. *I am **sealing** this letter shut.* 2. A **seal** is an ocean animal with thick, smooth fur and webbed feet to help it swim. A **seal** makes a barking sound.

search

(searches, searched, searching)
If you **search** for something, you look for it. *I am **searching** for my lost ring.*

seat

A **seat** is a place where you can sit. *Two children sit together on the **seat** on the school bus.*

second

1. A **second** is a very tiny amount of time. There are 60 **seconds** in a minute.
2. **Second** means the next one after the first. *You came in **second** in the race.*

A B C D E F G H I J K L M N O P Q R S T U V W X Y Z

secret

A **secret** is something that only a few people know about. *I can't tell you about the surprise because it is a **secret**.*

see

(sees, saw, seen, seeing)
When you use your eyes to look at something, you **see** it. *Did you **see** the pretty flower?*

seed

A **seed** is a little part of a plant that grows into a new plant if you put it in the ground. Most **seeds** have a hard shell to keep the tiny new plant inside safe. You can eat some **seeds,** like pumpkin **seeds.**

seem

(seems, seemed, seeming)
To **seem** means to look like or feel like something. *When you take a bath, it **seems** like you are swimming.*

seesaw

A **seesaw** is a big playground toy with a long, flat board. People sit on each end of the **seesaw** to move it up and down.

sell

(sells, sold, selling)
If someone **sells** you something, they give it to you when you pay them money.

send

(sends, sent, sending)
When you **send** something somewhere, you make it go to that place. *When the slugger hit a home run, he **sent** the baseball out of the park.*

sentence

A **sentence** is a group of words that make a complete thought. A written **sentence** starts with a capital letter and usually ends with a period.

September

September is a month of the year in the fall. *Labor Day is a holiday in **September**.*

service

1. A helpful act is a **service.** *Police officers perform a **service** to the neighborhood.* 2. A **service** is a type of ceremony or specific event. *Sunday, some people go to a church **service**.*

seven

Seven is a number that is one more than six. 6+1=7.

seventeen

Seventeen is a number that is one more than sixteen. 16+1=17.

seventy

Seventy is a number that is seven groups of 10. 10+10+10+10+10+10+10=70.

several

Several of something means there are more than two but fewer than many. *We will stay at camp for **several** days.*

shadow

A **shadow,** or a shaded area, appears where light is blocked. *When the sun shines on your face, your **shadow** is behind you.*

shake

(shakes, shook, shaken, shaking)
When you **shake** something, you move it up and down or side to side.

shampoo

Shampoo is a kind of soap you use to wash your hair. When you rub **shampoo** in your hair, it makes bubbles.

shape

Something's **shape** is the way it looks on the outside. Circles, squares, and triangles are some kinds of **shapes.**

share

(shares, sharing, shared)
If you let someone have a part of something or use something with you, you are **sharing.** *I will **share** my toys with you.*

shark

A **shark** is a large gray ocean fish with a wide mouth filled with sharp teeth. **Sharks** attack other fish.

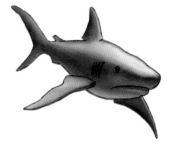

A B C D E F G H I J K L M N O P Q R S T U V W X Y Z

sharp
(sharper, sharpest)
If something is **sharp,** it has an edge or a point that is good for cutting. A knife and scissors are tools that are **sharp.**

she
She means a girl or a woman. **She** is wearing a dress.

sheep
(sheep)
A **sheep** is a farm animal with thick wool or hair. **Sheep** make a baaa, baaa sound.

sheet
1. A **sheet** is a big piece of cloth that you put on a bed. 2. A **sheet** is a thin, flat piece of paper.

shelf
(shelves)
A **shelf** is a long, flat piece of wood nailed to the wall to hold things. You can put books on the **shelf** in your bedroom.

shell
A **shell** is a hard cover that protects the soft things inside of it. Eggs, nuts, and turtles have **shells.**

ship
A **ship** is a very large boat that carries people and loads of things over the ocean, huge lakes, and big rivers.

shirt
A **shirt** is something you wear on the top part of your body. Most **shirts** have sleeves to cover your arms and buttons down the front.

shoe
A **shoe** is something you wear on your foot to keep it warm or protect it. You slide your foot in and buckle, snap, zip, or tie a **shoe.**

shop
(shops, shopped, shopping)
1. When you **shop,** you buy things. I **shopped** for new shoes.
2. A **shop** is a place, like a store, where you buy things. I went to the candy **shop** to buy lollipops.

short
(shorter, shortest)
1. If something is **short,** it is not very long. *The cat has a **short** tail.* 2. If someone is **short,** he is not tall.

shortly
Shortly means in a small amount of time. *We will leave **shortly** for the dentist's office.*

shorts
Shorts are pants that usually end above the knees. You wear **shorts** when the weather is warm.

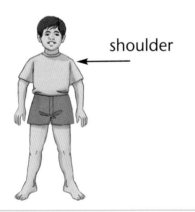

shoulder
Your **shoulder** is the highest part of your arm.

shoulder

shout
(shouts, shouted, shouting)
When you **shout,** you talk very loudly. *The bus driver **shouts** to be heard over the engine.*

shovel
A **shovel** is a digging tool with a long handle on one end and a curved piece on the other end to pick up things. You use a **shovel** to dig a hole in the dirt.

show
(shows, showed, shown, showing)
1. If you **show** someone something, you let her see it. *I am **showing** you my big toe.* 2. When you explain how to do something to somebody, you **show** them. *I will **show** you how to use the computer.* 3. If you go to a **show,** you are going to the movies.

shut
(shuts, shut, shutting)
When you **shut** something, you move it so it is closed. *I don't want the door open, so I will **shut** it.*

shy
(shier, shiest)
If someone is **shy,** he may feel a little afraid or hold back and not join in right away. *The little boy sat by himself at the party because he was **shy.***

A B C D E F G H I J K L M N O P Q R S T U V W X Y Z

sick

(sicker, sickest)
When you are **sick,** you do not feel well. *When the baby was **sick,** Daddy took her to the doctor.*

side

1. The **sides** of something are the outer edges or flat parts. *A room has four **sides,** but a window only has two **sides.*** 2. In games, the **sides** are the teams playing against each other. *In the football game, the blue **side** scored the points.*

sidewalk

A **sidewalk** is a paved path on the side of a road or going to someone's house. *You can ride on the **sidewalk** with your scooter.*

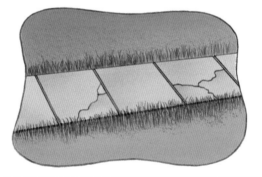

sight

You use the **sight** in your eyes to see or look at things. **Sight** is one of the five human senses.

sign

(signs, signed, signing)
1. When you **sign** something, you write your name on it. 2. A **sign** has pictures or words that tell you something. *If you see a red **sign** with the letters STOP, you must stop your car.* 3. A **sign** is a shape that means something. *The + **sign** means to add things together.*

silly

(sillier, silliest)
If you say or do something that is **silly,** you are being funny. Sometimes, when people don't think carefully about what they are doing, they can be **silly** by accident. *Wearing your shoes on the wrong feet is **silly.***

silver

Silver is a gray, shiny metal. Some coins and jewelry are made from **silver.**

since

Since means from that time. *We have been waiting for you to come to the picnic **since** one o'clock.*

sing

(sings, sang, sung, singing)
When you **sing,** you use your voice to make music.

sink
(sinks, sank, sunk, sinking)
1. When you **sink** something, it goes under water. *A heavy rock **sinks** in the water.* 2. A **sink** is a place where you wash things, like dishes or your hands.

sister
A **sister** is a girl who has the same mother or father as you.

sit
(sits, sat, sitting)
When you **sit,** you rest with your bottom on something. *The boy **sits** on the chair.*

six
Six is a number that is one more than five. 5+1=6.

6

sixteen
Sixteen is a number that is one more than fifteen. 15+1=16.

16

sixty
Sixty means six groups of ten.
10+10+10+10+10+10=60.

60

size
The **size** of something tells you how big it is. *What **size** shoes do you wear?*

skate
A **skate** is a special kind of shoe. A roller **skate** has wheels that roll over flat surfaces, while an ice **skate** has a thin, sharp, metal blade that slides over ice.

skateboard
A **skateboard** is a low, flat board with wheels on the bottom. You ride a **skateboard** with one foot while pushing the other foot off the ground. *Some **skateboard** riders can spin and jump with the board.*

skeleton
A **skeleton** is the set of bones inside your body that connect together and give your body its shape. Your **skeleton** protects your soft insides.

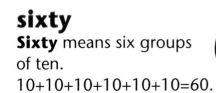

skin
1. **Skin** is what covers the outside of your body. 2. **Skin** is the outside layer of many fruits and vegetables. *You can peel the yellow **skin** of the banana.*

A B C D E F G H I J K L M N O P Q R S T U V W X Y Z

skinny
(skinnier, skinniest)
If someone or something is **skinny,** that person or thing is thin. *A green bean is a **skinny** vegetable.*

skirt
A **skirt** is a piece of clothing that girls and women wear. A **skirt** goes around the waist and hangs down, covering up part of the legs.

skull
Your **skull** is the round bone of your head that protects your brain.

skunk
A **skunk** is a small wild animal with a long, black-and-white-striped, furry tail. A frightened **skunk** squirts a bad-smelling spray.

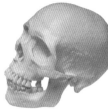

sky
(skies)
The **sky** is the space above the ground where you see the clouds and sun during the day and the stars and moon at night.

sled
A **sled** is something you sit on to ride on the snow. **Sleds** have smooth bottoms or two thin metal blades that help them slide along.

sleep
(sleeps, slept, sleeping)
When you **sleep,** you close your eyes and rest your whole body and mind. People usually **sleep** at night in a bed.

slide
(slides, slid, sliding)
1. When something **slides,** it moves along easily. *You just **slide** along on the ice.*
2. A **slide** is a long, smooth ramp that leans against a ladder on the playground. You climb the ladder, sit on the **slide,** then zip down it.

slow
(slower, slowest)
If something is **slow,** it takes a long time to go someplace or do something. *The tractor was very **slow** as it pulled a heavy load.*

small
(smaller, smallest)
If somebody or something is **small,** it is not very big. *A violet is a **small** plant.*

smart
(smarter, smartest)
Someone who is **smart** is bright and uses her brain to know things. *A **smart** boy does not play with matches.*

smile

(smiles, smiled, smiling)
1. When you **smile,** the corners of your mouth turn up. 2. A **smile** is a look your face makes when you are happy.

smoke

Smoke is a cloud of gray gas that rises from burning things, such as a campfire. You can see and smell **smoke.**

snack

A **snack** is a little something you can eat quickly in between meals. A piece of fruit or crackers and cheese are healthy **snacks.**

snail

A **snail** is a small animal with a hard shell on its back and no legs. A **snail** slides along very slowly.

snake

A **snake** is a long, thin reptile without legs. A **snake** wiggles along by sliding over the ground.

sneakers

Sneakers are cloth or leather shoes with rubber on the bottoms. People wear **sneakers** to play sports where they need to run fast.

snow

Snow is water that has frozen into tiny pieces and falls from the sky. During very cold weather, white **snow** sometimes covers the ground. *We made the **snow** into snowballs.*

so

So means very or highly. *This soda tastes **so** sweet.*

soap

Soap is something you use with water to wash and clean things, like dishes or your hands. **Soap** comes in bars, liquids, or powders.

soccer

Soccer is a game where two teams try to kick a ball into a big net.

A B C D E F G H I J K L M N O P Q R S T U V W X Y Z

sock

A **sock** is something soft that you wear on your foot under your shoes.

soda

Soda is a sweet drink with fizzy bubbles in it.

soft

(softer, softest)

If something feels **soft,** it is not scratchy or hard. *A pillow is soft.*

softball

In the game of **softball,** one team tries to hit a white ball with a bat while the other team tries to catch it. **Softball** players try to score points by running around the bases.

soldier

A **soldier** is a person who is trained to fight in an army to protect her country.

some

Some means an amount, such as a few of something. *The chicken laid* **some** *eggs.*

somebody

Somebody means an unnamed person. **Somebody** *left the door open.*

someone

Someone means somebody or an unnamed person. *I see* **someone** *on the skateboard.*

something

Something means an unnamed being, material, or act. *The boy was hungry and wanted to eat* **something.**

sometimes

Sometimes means now and then. **Sometimes,** *the mommy and daughter play a game of softball.*

somewhere

Somewhere means in, at, or to an unnamed place. *The snake wiggled away* **somewhere.**

son

A **son** is a boy or a man who is somebody's child.

song

A **song** is a piece of music. Many **songs** have words that you can sing. *The kids are singing a* **song.**

soon

(sooner, soonest)

If something is happening **soon,** it will happen not very long from now. *The airplane will be taking off very **soon.***

sorry

(sorrier, sorriest)

If you feel **sorry,** you are very sad about something that happened. *I am **sorry** you broke your foot.*

sound

A **sound** is something you can hear. *When the boy plays the drum, it makes a loud **sound.***

soup

Soup is a hot liquid food. Sometimes **soup** can have meat or vegetables in it. *We had tomato **soup** with crackers for lunch today.*

south

South is a direction that is on your right side when you watch the sun come up in the morning.

space

1. **Space** is a place with nothing in it. *There is a lot of **space** inside an empty bag.* 2. **Space** is the huge area that is everything outside Earth. **Space** is where the stars and planets are.

spaghetti

Spaghetti is a long, thin, stringy pasta. People eat **spaghetti** with sauces, like tomato or cheese, on top.

speak

(speaks, spoke, spoken, speaking)

When you **speak** to someone, you say something. *The girl **speaks** to her teacher about her project.*

special

1. If something is **special,** it is more important or better than something else. *My birthday is **special** because it only happens once a year.* 2. If something is **special,** it is made for a particular job. *The dentist has a **special** tool to drill my teeth.*

speed

(speeds, sped, speeding)

If someone or something **speeds,** that person or thing is in a big hurry and moves very fast. *The train is **speeding** past the towns.*

spell
(spells, spelled, spelling)
1. When you **spell** a word, you say or write the letters in order. C-A-T *spells* cat. 2. In stories or movies, a **spell** is a set of special words that make magic happen. *The fairy princess said "Hocus Pocus" and put a **spell** on the sleeping cat to make him jump in the air.*

spider
A **spider** is a small creature with eight legs and no wings. A **spider** spins a sticky web to catch other tiny animals for food.

spill
(spills, spilled, spilling)
A **spill** is what happens when something drops or pours out of its container. Most **spills** are not meant to happen, like **spilling** your milk.

spin
(spins, spun, spinning)
When something **spins,** it turns around very fast. *The dancer **spins** around on her toes.*

spinach
Spinach is a vegetable that grows in bunches of dark, green leaves. You can eat **spinach** raw or cooked.

splash
(splashes, splashed, splashing)
To **splash** somebody means to make them wet with liquid. *The baby **splashed** his yellow rubber duck with water in the bathtub.*

sponge
A **sponge** is something soft with little holes in it that cleans up wet spills. You can also wet a **sponge** to wipe away messes.

spoon
A **spoon** is a tool with a long handle and a small round bowl used for eating. You can eat soft or runny food, like ice cream or soup, with a **spoon.**

sport

A **sport** is a game that exercises your body to help it stay healthy. **Sports,** such as baseball or tennis, are played for fun.

spot

1. A **spot** is a small round mark. A ladybug has black **spots.** 2. A **spot** is also a small place. *This flat rock is a good spot for our picnic.*

spring

(springs, sprang, sprung, springing)
1. If something **springs** out, it jumps. *The tiger springs out of the bushes.*
2. **Spring** is the season of the year between winter and summer. Flowers start to bloom in **spring.** 3. A **spring** is a curly piece of metal that pops back into place when you touch it.

square

A **square** is a shape with four straight sides of the same length and four even corners.

squirrel

A **squirrel** is a small gray, brown, black, or red animal with a long fluffy tail. **Squirrels** eat nuts and live in nests they build in trees.

stamp

A **stamp** is a small piece of paper with a picture on it. The **stamp** has a sticky side to put on a letter to mail.

stand

(stands, stood, standing)
When you **stand** somewhere, you are up on your feet. *I am standing in line to buy a movie ticket.*

star

1. A **star** is a bright light of burning gas that you see in the sky at night. 2. A **star** is a shape with five or six points. Sometimes your teacher puts a **star** shape on top of your paper if you do a good job. 3. A **star** is someone famous, like a person in movies or TV.

starfish

(starfish)
A **starfish** is a sea animal that is not really a fish. A **starfish** has five arms that stick out of its body like the points of a star.

A B C D E F G H I J K L M N O P Q R S T U V W X Y Z

start

(starts, started, starting)
When you **start** something, you begin, or do the first part of it. *When I **start** to bake cookies, I heat the oven first.*

state

(states, stated, stating)
1. If you **state** something, you use words to tell someone about it. 2. A **state** is a small part of a country with its own people, land, and laws. *The **state** of Texas is in the southern part of the United States.*

stay

(stays, stayed, staying)
When you **stay** someplace, you remain there and do not go away. *People usually **stay** inside when it's raining.*

steep

(steeper, steepest)
If something, like a mountain, is **steep,** it slants a lot and is very hard to climb.

stem

A **stem** is the long part of a plant that grows out of the ground. Roots, branches, and flowers grow from **stems.**

stem

step

1. A **step** is something you stand on to make you taller to reach things. Many **steps** in a row are called a staircase.
2. When you take a **step,** you lift up your foot and put it down in another place.

stick

(sticks, stuck, sticking)
1. When you **stick** things together, you join them with glue or tape. 2. When you **stick** something with a pointed object, like a pin, you push it in. *The doctor **sticks** you with a needle when she gives you a shot.* 3. A **stick** is a long, thin piece of wood.

sticker

A **sticker** is a gummed label with words, numbers, or pictures, much like a stamp. People collect pretty colored **stickers** and stick them in a book.

sticky

(stickier, stickiest)
If something is **sticky,** it has a type of glue on it so it will join or stick to another thing. *The **sticky** tape holds the picture on the wall.*

still
(stiller, stillest)
1. If someone or something is **still,** it is not moving. *The deer stood **still** in the woods.* 2. If something is **still** happening, it has not yet stopped. *Even though it feels a little warmer, it is **still** snowing outside.*

stomach
Your **stomach** is the place inside of your body where your food goes to digest when you eat it.

stone
A **stone** is a small piece of a hard rock that comes in many colors. You can sometimes find **stones** on beaches.

stool
A **stool** is a type of chair with legs and a seat but no back. **Stools** can be tall or short.

stop
(stops, stopped, stopping)
1. If you **stop** what you are doing, you do not do it any more. ***Stop** blowing up the balloon, or it will pop.* 2. If something that is moving **stops,** it stands still. *The car **stopped** for the traffic light.*

stop sign
A **stop sign** is red with the word *STOP* painted on it in white. A **stop sign** is placed where roads cross so drivers will not crash their cars into each other.

store
(stores, stored, storing)
1. When you **store** something, you put it away in case you need it at another time. *I **stored** your mittens away in a box until winter.* 2. A **store** is a place where people buy things.

story
(stories)
A **story** tells you about things that have happened. Some **stories** are real, while others are make-believe.

stove
A **stove** is a machine that cooks food. The top of the **stove** has burners, and the inside has an oven.

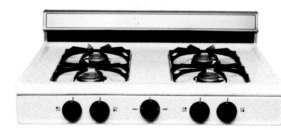

A B C D E F G H I J K L M N O P Q R S T U V W X Y Z

strange
(stranger, strangest)
If something is **strange,** it is not what you expected it to be. *The cheese has a very **strange** smell to it.*

stranger
If someone is a **stranger,** she is a person who you do not know. *You must never get in the car with a **stranger.***

straw
A **straw** is a thin tube that you drink through. When you sip on a **straw,** you pull liquid into your mouth.

strawberry
(strawberries)
A **strawberry** is a small, soft red fruit with tiny seeds all over it. ***Strawberry** shortcake is a favorite summer dessert.*

street
A **street** is a road in a city or town that usually has buildings along each side.

string
1. **String** is a long, thin, ropelike material that people use to tie things together, such as packages. 2. Musical instruments, like a guitar, have wire **strings** that make sounds when your fingers tug at them.

strong
(stronger, strongest)
1. If you are very **strong,** you are quite powerful. *The man is so **strong** he can pick up two heavy suitcases.* 2. If something is **strong,** it is hard to break it. *A bulldozer is a **strong** machine made out of metal.*

study
(studies, studied, studying)
When you **study,** you learn about something. *The girl **studies** the pictures in her book to find out more about different birds.*

subject
A **subject** is something you study or discuss. *Math is a **subject** in school.*

subtract

(subtracts, subtracted, subtracting)
When you **subtract,** you take one number away from another number. *If you **subtract** the number three from the number five, you have two left.*

such

1. **Such** means something has a particular quality. *The baby is **such** a happy little boy that he smiles all of the time.* 2. **Such** means like or similar to. *The girl wants something hot to drink, **such** as soup.*

suck

(sucks, sucked, sucking)
If someone **sucks** on something, she pulls in liquid with her mouth. *The baby **sucks** on the bottle to drink some milk.*

sugar

Sugar is a grainy brown or white food that makes things sweet. Soda, candy, and icing have **sugar** in them.

suit

A **suit** is an outfit of matching clothes. A **suit** has a jacket and pants or a skirt.

summer

Summer is the hottest season of the year. **Summer** comes between spring and fall. *Our family went to the beach last **summer.***

sun

The **sun** is the big, bright, yellowish star you see in the sky during the day. The **sun** keeps us warm and gives us light.

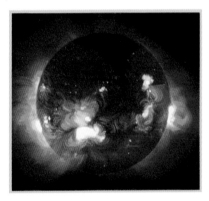

sundae

A **sundae** is a dessert in a dish with ice cream and tasty things sprinkled on the top. Ice cream **sundaes** can come with fruit, nuts, whipped cream, and sauce.

A B C D E F G H I J K L M N O P Q R S T U V W X Y Z

Sunday

Sunday is the first day of the week. Some people go to church on **Sunday**, while others like to relax on this weekend day.

sunglasses

You wear **sunglasses** on your face during sunny days to protect your eyes. The lenses in **sunglasses** are made of dark or colored plastic or glass.

sunny

(sunnier, sunniest)
It is **sunny** outside when the sun is shining brightly. *Our family likes to go to the beach on a **sunny** day.*

sure

If you are **sure** about something, you know that you are right. *I am **sure** the sun will set at six o'clock today.*

surprise

A **surprise** is something you did not know was going to happen.

swallow

(swallows, swallowed, swallowing)
When you **swallow** something that you eat or drink, it goes down your throat into your stomach.

sweater

A **sweater** is something you wear on the top part of your body and arms to  keep you very warm. Some **sweaters** have buttons, while other sweaters pull over your head.

sweet

(sweeter, sweetest)
1. If a food or drink is **sweet**, it tastes like sugar. Candy is **sweet.** 2. If you say someone is very **sweet**, you think she is being kind. *You are very **sweet** to push the little girl on the swing.*

swim

(swims, swam, swimming)
When you **swim,** you use your arms and legs to move yourself through the water.

swing

(swings, swung, swinging)
1. When something **swings,** it moves back and forth in the air.  *The weight on the tall grandfather clock **swings** as it goes* tick-tock. 2. A **swing** is a seat on the playground that hangs on two chains and moves back and forth when you move your legs.

table

A **table** is a piece of furniture with a flat top and four legs. You sit on a chair at the **table** to eat a meal.

taco

You make a **taco** by folding a thin tortilla around a spicy mixture of meat and cheese topped with vegetables. The tortilla for the **taco** can be made with flour or corn. The **taco** tortilla can be soft or crunchy. You eat a **taco** with your hands.

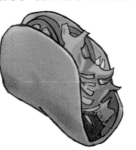

tag

1. **Tag** is a game where one player runs after the others and tries to tap them.
2. A **tag** is a label that has information printed on it. *The **tag** sewn in the dress gives the size.*

tail

A **tail** grows out of the back end of some animals' bodies. Animals use their **tails** for moving, showing feelings, and holding things. *The dog wagged its **tail** to say hello.*

take

(takes, took, taken, taking)
If you **take** something, you move it or carry it away. *The dog **took** the bone to eat it in the doghouse.*

talk

(talks, talked, talking)
When you **talk,** you say something. *The girl **talked** to her friend on the telephone.*

tall

(taller, tallest)
If someone or something is **tall,** it is very high above the ground. *The basketball player was so **tall** he could touch the basket.*

tap

(taps, tapped, tapping)
When you **tap** something, you hit it gently. *My teacher **taps** his fingers on the top of his desk.*

tape

1. A **tape** is a long strip of plastic, cloth, or paper with a sticky material on one side. You use

tape to hold things together or hang a poster on the wall. 2. People record words and pictures on **tape**. This **tape** is a narrow strip of plastic in a case called a cassette. *I will play a **tape** on my **tape** recorder of my friend singing a song.*

tape measure

A **tape measure** is a long bendable ruler made out of plastic, cloth, or metal. Carpenters and people who sew keep a **tape measure** in their pocket so they can use it to see how long things are.

taste

(tastes, tasted, tasting)
When you **taste** food, you put it in your mouth to see what flavor it is. *The baker **tasted** the frosting before putting it on the cake.*

tea

Tea is a drink you make by pouring hot water over special dried leaves. You can

add sugar, lemon, or milk to **tea,** which can be served hot or cold.

teach

(teaches, taught, teaching)
When you **teach** someone, you help that person learn new things. *My big brother is **teaching** me how to hold a baseball bat.*

teacher

A **teacher** is a person whose job is to help others learn things. Most **teachers** work in schools.

team

A **team** is a group of people who play sports together on the same side. *The orange soccer **team** scored a goal.*

teapot

A **teapot** has a handle and a spout for pouring tea.

teddy bear

A **teddy bear** is a soft, cuddly toy that looks like a bear. Many children like to take their **teddy bears** to bed with them.

telephone

A **telephone** is a machine for talking to and listening to people who are far away. A **telephone** rings to let you know someone is calling you.

television

A **television** is a machine that picks up air waves and turns them into pictures and sounds. You might watch the news, cartoons, or a movie on **television.** TV is the short name for **television.**

tell

(tells, told, telling)
If you **tell** someone something, you say what you know about it. *The girl is **telling** her friend about the television show.*

temple

A **temple** is a place where people go to worship their god.

ten

Ten is a number that is one more than nine. 9+1=10. *You have **ten** toes on your feet.*

tennis

In the game of **tennis,** players try to hit a ball over a net with racquets. **Tennis** is played on a hard court where the ball will bounce.

tepee

A **tepee** is a tent shaped like a cone and made from animal skins or fabric placed around poles. Some Native Americans lived in **tepees** a long time ago.

terrible

Something that is **terrible** is very bad. *A **terrible** fire burned down the house.*

than

Than is used when you are comparing things. *My kite flies higher **than** your kite.*

thank

(thanks, thanked, thanking)
When you **thank** people, you tell them how happy you are with something they did. *The old lady **thanked** the girl for shoveling the snow from her path.*

Thanksgiving

Thanksgiving is a holiday that happens in the United States every year on the fourth Thursday in November. **Thanksgiving** reminds you to be glad for the good things in your life. Many families share a turkey dinner on **Thanksgiving.**

A B C D E F G H I J K L M N O P Q R S T U V W X Y Z

that

1. **That** means a specific thing. 2. **That** refers to something that is not close to you. *I am going to run to **that** tree way over there.*

the

The means a specific one. ***The** girl wants to eat **the** plum.*

their

Their means that something belongs to them. *The boys hung up **their** coats.*

them

Them means two or more people or things. *The three boxes belong to **them**.*

then

Then means something happens at that time. *When you finish your lunch, **then** you will meet me at the swimming pool.*

there

There means in, at, or to that place. *Please go over **there** by the chair, and wait for me.*

these

These means things that are close. ***These** pink mittens on the table are mine.*

they

They is a word you use when you are talking about more than one person or thing. ***They** are going to share the large pizza for dinner.*

thin

(thinner, thinnest)
1. If something is **thin,** it is not very wide. *The girl's hair ribbon is **thin.*** 2. If someone or something is **thin,** that person or thing does not weigh very much and is not fat. *The woman is **thin.***

thing

A **thing** is any object or event you can think about, see, touch, or do. *The girl wants to hold the big purple **thing** when she goes to the circus.*

think

(thinks, thought, thinking)
1. When you **think** about something, you use your mind. *The girl is **thinking** of an answer to the question.* 2. **Think** can also mean to believe something is true. *I **think** I know how to fix the car.*

third

Third means the next one after the second one. *My friend in the yellow hat is the **third** one in line for the donuts.*

thirteen

Thirteen is a number that is one more than twelve. 12+1=13. Some people think **thirteen** is an unlucky number.

thirty

Thirty is a number that means three groups of ten. 10+10+10=30.

this

This means one that is close or near by. *This blanket is keeping me warm.*

those

Those means specific things that are not close to you. *Those balls are full of air and very bouncy!*

though

Though means in spite of the fact. *The lady is still cold, even **though** she is wearing her sweater.*

thought

A **thought** is an idea that you have. *The teacher **thought** she would take the children outside to play on this sunny day.*

thousand

A **thousand** is a number that is ten times one hundred. 10×100=1,000.

three

Three is a number that stands for one more than two. 2+1=3. *People eat **three** meals a day.*

throat

Your **throat** is the part of your body that is at the back of your mouth. When you swallow something, it goes down your **throat.**

through

If you go **through** something, you go in one side and out another. *The train went **through** the tunnel.*

throw

(throws, threw, thrown, throwing)
When you **throw** something, you make it move through the air with your hand. *The boy **throws** the paper airplane up high.*

thumb

Your **thumb** is the shortest of your five fingers. You pick up things between your **thumb** and fingers.

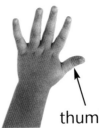

thumb

A B C D E F G H I J K L M N O P Q R S T U V W X Y Z

Thursday

Thursday is the fifth day of the week. **Thursday** comes after Wednesday.

ticket

A **ticket** is a small piece of paper that shows you have paid for something. You need a **ticket** to go to the movies.

tie

(ties, tied, tying)
1. When you **tie** something together, you fasten it by wrapping and knotting ribbon or string. *The girl **ties** her shoes.*
2. A **tie** is a thin strip of cloth that hangs down the front of a man's shirt when he is dressed up.

tiger

A **tiger** is a jungle animal that looks like a big cat with orange fur and black stripes.

tight

(tighter, tightest)
If something is **tight,** it does not have a loose, easy fit. *The boy's mother tied his shoes **tight** so they wouldn't come off.*

time

1. **Time** is how long something takes to happen. **Time** is measured in seconds, minutes, hours, days, weeks, months, and years. 2. **Time** is the hours and minutes shown on a clock. *The **time** is three o'clock.*

tip

(tips, tipped, tipping)
1. To **tip** something over means to push it so it leans. *The boy **tips** the toy box over and things begin to fall out.*
2. The **tip** of something is the pointed end of it. *The **tip** of the mountain has snow on it.*

tire

A **tire** is a circle of rubber that fits over a wheel and is usually filled with air. Cars and bikes ride on **tires.**

to

To usually means in the direction of someone or something. *My mother sent me **to** the store.*

toad

A **toad** is a small brown-and-green animal that looks like a frog with thick, bumpy skin. A **toad** uses two large back legs to hop on land.

toast

Toast is a kind of brown, crispy bread cooked in a toaster. People make **toast** by heating it, and then they sometimes put butter and jam on it.

toaster

A **toaster** is a small machine that cooks bread. Each opening in the top of the **toaster** holds one slice.

today

Today means at the present day or time. *Today I am going to go to the tennis match.*

toe

A **toe** is one of the five small parts that is at the end of your foot.

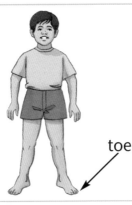

toe

together

Together means with another person or thing. *The two friends ate lunch together at the fast-food restaurant.*

toilet

A **toilet** is a special bowl with a seat that you sit on to go to the bathroom. You flush a **toilet** when you are finished using it.

tomato

(tomatoes)

A **tomato** is a juicy, round, red fruit that grows on a vine. You can eat a **tomato** raw or cooked in a salad, sandwich, soup, or sauce.

tomorrow

Tomorrow means the day after today. *The mail carrier will bring the package to you tomorrow.*

tongue

Your **tongue** is the soft, moving, pink part inside your mouth. Your **tongue** helps you to taste things, swallow food, and speak.

tonight

Tonight is the night or the evening of this day. *We are going to hear a bedtime story tonight.*

too

Too means in addition. *The children want to come along in the sailboat, too.*

A B C D E F G H I J K L M N O P Q R S T U V W X Y Z

tool

A **tool** is something you use to do work, such as a hammer. You can hold most **tools** in your hand.

toolbox

(toolboxes)

A **toolbox** is a special chest for storing and carrying tools, such as screwdrivers and drills.

tooth

(teeth)

A **tooth** is a hard, white thing in your mouth that you use for biting and chewing.

toothache

A **toothache** is a pain that you get in your tooth. If you eat too much sugary food, like candy, you might get a **toothache.**

toothbrush

(toothbrushes)

A **toothbrush** has a long handle with bristles on one end. You put toothpaste on a **toothbrush** to clean your teeth after you eat.

toothpaste

Toothpaste is a cleaner for your teeth that comes in tubes. You squeeze thick, creamy **toothpaste** onto your brush.

top

1. A **top** is a toy with a pointed end that spins around. 2. A **top** is a cover for a jar or something that covers the upper part of your body. *You screw the top on a bottle of soda.* 3. The **top** is the highest part of something. *The girl climbs to the top of the jungle gym.*

touch

(touches, touched, touching)

1. If you **touch** something, you feel it with your hand. 2. When two things **touch,** this means there is no space between them. *When a book is closed, the pages touch each other.*

toward

Toward means to go in the direction of something. *The farmer quickly walked toward his cow.*

towel

A **towel** is a large, thick, soft cloth you use to dry yourself after taking a bath.

town

A **town** is a place with lots of streets, houses, buildings, and stores where many people live and work.

toy

A **toy** is something you play with to have fun. Dolls, balls, and games are **toys.**

toy box

(toy boxes)
A **toy box** is a container that

holds toys, like balls, blocks, and stuffed animals. When you clean up toys, you can put them in the **toy box.**

track

1. A **track** is a path where people race or jog with their feet. 2. A railroad **track** is a special road where trains run over metal rails to get somewhere.

trade

(trades, traded, trading)
When you **trade** something with someone, you exchange or swap things. *The boys **traded** their baseball cards.*

traffic light

A **traffic light** is a series of colored lights beside a road that tells drivers what to do: red means to stop, yellow means to slow down, and green means to go.

trailer

A **trailer** is a vehicle with wheels but without a motor that attaches to a car or truck to help you move things to another place. *A **trailer** could hold milk in a large, long tank.*

train

(trains, trained, training)
1. If you **train** your pet, you teach it how to do something. *I **trained** my dog to catch a stick.* 2. You can travel on tracks in a **train** pulled by an engine.

trap

A **trap** is something that you set to catch an animal or a person. *You put cheese on a **trap** to catch a mouse.*

trash

Trash is something that is not any good, like junk or garbage, that people throw away. *The man threw his paper cup in the **trash.***

trash can

A **trash can** is a large container made of metal or plastic with a lid. You throw garbage in a **trash can.**

A B C D E F G H I J K L M N O P Q R S T U V W X Y Z

travel

(travels, traveled, traveling)
When you **travel,** you go from one place to another. *I **traveled** to school on the yellow school bus.*

tray

A **tray** is a shallow, flat board used for holding or carrying objects. *The child carried her food on a **tray.***

treasure

A **treasure** is a large number of things of value, like gold, jewelry, or coins. *Pirates hid their special things in a **treasure** chest.*

tree

A **tree** is a tall, woody plant with a trunk and branches. Some trees have leaves, while others have needles.

triangle

A **triangle** is a shape with three straight sides and three corners.

trick

(tricks, tricked, tricking)
1. **Trick** means to play a prank on others to try to fool them. *The boy **tricked** his mom by hiding her car keys so they couldn't leave the park.* 2. A **trick** is a prank on someone.

tricycle

A **tricycle** is a toy with three wheels and a seat that you ride. You pedal a **tricycle** and steer it with a handlebar.

trip

(trips, tripped, tripping)
1. When you **trip,** your foot bumps into something, and you fall down. *My father **tripped** over the sleeping cat.*
2. When you go on a **trip,** you travel somewhere.

trombone

A **trombone** is a long, curved, brass musical instrument that makes a sound when you blow into it. One end of the **trombone** slides in and out.

trophy

(trophies)
A **trophy** is a prize you get when you win a game or race. Sometimes a **trophy** has your name on it.

trouble

If you have **trouble** doing something, it may be difficult because there are problems. *The boys were having **trouble** fishing because they ran out of worms.*

troublemaker

Someone who is a **troublemaker** behaves badly. A **troublemaker** creates problems for others.

truck

A **truck** is a big vehicle with large wheels that carries things in the back. A driver rides in the front of a **truck.**

true

(truer, truest)
1. If something is **true,** it really happened. 2. **True** means right or correct. *It is **true** that a night comes after every day.*

trumpet

A **trumpet** is a curved, brass instrument that makes a sound when you blow into it. You push three valves on the **trumpet** to change the sounds it makes.

trunk

1. A **trunk** is a large, heavy box that people use to store things. 2. An elephant's long nose is called a **trunk,** and the animal uses it to get food and water. 3. The **trunk** of a tree is the long, thick part that comes up from the ground.

trust

(trusts, trusted, trusting)
If you **trust** someone, you believe they will do what they say. *I **trust** my friend to care for my pet.*

try

(tries, tried, trying)
1. If you **try** something, you are testing it out. *I **tried** the salad to see if I liked it.*
2. When you **try** to do something, you attempt to do it. *I **try** to help my mom.*

T-shirt

A **T-shirt** is something with short-sleeves that covers the top of your body. Many **T-shirts** have words or pictures on them.

tub

A **tub** is a wide, round metal or plastic container. You can carry things in a **tub,** or you can put water in it to wash things.

tuba

A **tuba** is a huge brass instrument that makes low sounds when you blow into it.

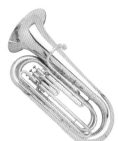

A B C D E F G H I J K L M N O P Q R S T U V W X Y Z

Tuesday

Tuesday is the third day of the week. **Tuesday** comes after Monday.

tug

(tugs, tugged, tugging)
When you **tug** on something, you pull very hard to move it. *I am **tugging** on my dog's collar to bring him inside.*

tugboat

A **tugboat** is a powerful boat that pulls other boats safely into the harbor. Some **tugboats** pull barges over the river.

tune

A tune is the melody of a song. When someone sings or plays a musical instrument, you hear the **tune.**

turkey

A **turkey** is a big bird that can raise its tail into a fan shape. **Turkeys** live on a farm or in the wild. People like to eat **turkey** at Thanksgiving.

turn

(turns, turned, turning)
1. When something **turns,** it goes around. *The wheels of a car **turn** when you drive it.* 2. When a thing **turns** into something else, it changes. *A tadpole **turns** into a frog.*

turtle

A **turtle** is an animal with wrinkly skin and a hard shell. A **turtle** can hide inside its shell.

twelve

Twelve is a number that is one more than eleven. 11+1=12. **Twelve** is also sometimes called a dozen, such as a dozen eggs.

twenty

Twenty is a number that is two groups of ten. 10+10=20.

two

Two is the number that comes after one. 1+1=2. *You have **two** eyes.*

umbrella

An **umbrella** has a round cloth or plastic top and a long handle with a curved end. You hold an **umbrella** over your head to stay dry when it rains.

umpire

An **umpire** is a person who makes sure the players follow the rules in sports, such as baseball.

uncertain

If something is **uncertain,** it may change at any time. *It is **uncertain** if the rain will stay away for our picnic.*

uncle

Your **uncle** is the brother of your father or your mother, or the husband of your aunt.

under

If something is **under** something else, it is below it. *The pear is **under** the two lemons.*

understand

(understands, understood, understanding)
If you **understand** something, you know what it means. *I **understand** the directions for building the toy race car.*

underwear

Underwear is clothing you wear under other clothes next to your skin. Underpants and undershirts are **underwear.**

unhappy

(unhappier, unhappiest)
If you are **unhappy,** you are sad or upset about something. *You are **unhappy** that your goldfish died.*

uniform

A **uniform** is a set of clothes that people wear to show they do a certain job or belong to a certain group. *Nurses, firefighters, athletes, and Brownies and Cub Scouts all wear **uniforms.***

until

Until means up to the time something happens. *The girl waited to cross the street **until** the traffic light changed.*

unzip

(unzips, unzipped, unzipping)
When you **unzip** something, you move the zipper along a track and open it up. *The lady **unzips** her sweater.*

up

If somebody or something goes **up,** it moves from a lower level to a higher one. *The airplane goes **up** in the sky.*

Uranus

Uranus is a planet in the solar system. **Uranus** is the third largest planet and seventh planet from the Sun.

us

Us is another way to say we. *Please give the tennis balls to **us.***

use

(uses, used, using)
When you **use** something, you are doing a job with it. *You **use** a hammer and nails to build a house.*

148

vacation

A **vacation** is a time off from work and school. A **vacation** is often a time for fun and trips.

vacuum cleaner

A **vacuum cleaner** is a machine that sucks up dirt. You use a **vacuum cleaner** to clean rugs, floors, and curtains.

valentine

A **valentine** is a greeting card that you send to people you like on Valentine's Day. *Many **valentines** have heart-shape designs.*

Valentine's Day

Valentine's Day is a holiday that takes place on February 14. On **Valentine's Day** you send cards, flowers, or candy to people you love.

vase

A **vase** is a tall, thin container made out of glass that holds water. You can put fresh flowers in a **vase.**

vegetable

A **vegetable** is a plant that you eat for food. Carrots, peas, and broccoli are **vegetables.**

Venus

Venus is the second planet from the Sun.

very

You use the word **very** before another word to make it show a greater amount. *The elephant is **very** big.*

vest

A **vest** is a sleeveless jacket worn on the top part of your body over a shirt. A **vest** can be part of a suit.

video camera

A **video camera** is something that records movies. You hold a **video camera** in your hand. Sometimes a **video camera** is called a camcorder.

videotape

A **videotape** is a special tape that records pictures and sounds. You use **videotape** in your VCR or camcorder.

view

A **view** is what you see from a particular place. *The **view** of the flowers from the top of the hill is beautiful.*

vine

A **vine** is a plant with a long, winding stem that grows along the ground or up trees. *Squash grows on a **vine**.*

violet

A **violet** is a small sweet-smelling flower with five petals. **Violets** are purple, white, yellow, or pink.

violin

A **violin** is a wooden instrument that has four strings. You play the **violin** by moving a bow across the strings.

visit

(visits, visited, visiting)
When you **visit** someone or something, you go to see that person or thing. *The girls are **visiting** the library to get books.*

voice

Your **voice** is the sound you make when you talk or sing.

volleyball

A **volleyball** is a round, white ball about the size of a soccer ball. You hit a **volleyball** over a net during the game of **volleyball.**

vulture

A **vulture** is a large bird that does not have any feathers on its head. **Vultures** eat animals that are already dead.

waffle

A **waffle** is a crisp, bumpy cake cooked in a waffle iron. *We had **waffles** with butter and syrup for breakfast.*

wag

(wags, wagged, wagging)
To **wag** means to move back and forth. *The dog was **wagging** his tail.*

wagon

A **wagon** carries people and things from place to place. **Wagons** can be pulled by hand, by horses, or by a tractor.

wait

(waits, waited, waiting)
If you **wait,** you stay in one place until something happens. *We **waited** by the toaster for the toast to pop up.*

walk

(walks, walked, walking)
When you **walk,** you put one foot in front of the other and move along.

wall

1. A **wall** is one side of a room. 2. A **wall** is something you make with stones or bricks to separate one person's land from another's.

wallet

A **wallet** is a small folder for money that you carry in your pocket or purse.

walnut

A **walnut** is a thick, hard-shelled nut from a tree. You can eat the soft, chewy nut inside.

wand

A **wand** is a small, thin stick you hold in your hand. A magician waves a **wand** to perform magic tricks.

want

(wants, wanted, wanting)
If you **want** something, you would like to have it. *The girl **wants** some peanut butter for her sandwich.*

A B C D E F G H I J K L M N O P Q R S T U V W X Y Z

war

When armies or groups of people fight against each other, they are at **war.**

warm

(warmer, warmest)
If you are **warm,** you are fairly hot and no longer cold. *The boy wears his fuzzy hat to keep his head **warm.***

was

(be, am, are, is, were, been, being)
Was means something occurred. *She **was** playing volleyball this morning.*

wash

(washes, washed, washing)
To **wash** is to clean something with soap and water. You **wash** your hands before you eat.

washcloth

A **washcloth** is a small square cloth you use to wash your face and body with soap and water.

waste

(wastes, wasted, wasting)
If you **waste** something, you are using more of it than you need. *Do not **waste** all of the toothpaste on your brush.*

watch

(watches, watched, watching)
1. When you **watch** someone or something, you look at that person or thing to see what is happening. *You **watch** the bee fly to the flower.* 2. A **watch** is a small clock you wear on your wrist.

water

Water is a clear liquid without any smell or taste. **Water** falls from the sky in the form of rain. You can drink **water** or take a bath in it.

watermelon

A **watermelon** is a large, juicy fruit with a thick green skin. Inside, the **watermelon** is crisp and pink with many seeds.

wave

(waves, waved, waving)
1. You say hello or good-bye to someone when you **wave** your hand side to side. 2. A **wave** is a high, curved line of water moving across the ocean. *The boy rides the surfboard on the **waves.***

way

1. The **way** you do something is how you do it. *This is the **way** you make the bed.* 2. A **way** is how you get from one place to another. *This is the **way** from my house to town.*

we

When the speaker includes others, she says **we.** *We went for a hike to the pond.*

wear

(wears, wore, worn, wearing)
1. When you **wear** clothes, they cover your body. *I am **wearing** my snowsuit and hat to play outdoors in the cold.* 2. If something **wears** out, it has been used a lot of times and is no longer as good or as strong. *The car tires went flat when they **wore** out.*

weather

The **weather** is what it is like outdoors: sunny, windy, hot, cold, or rainy. *I am wearing a bathing suit for the hot **weather.***

wedding

A **wedding** is a marriage ceremony and celebration when a man and a woman become husband and wife.

Wednesday

Wednesday is the fourth day of the week. **Wednesday** comes after Tuesday.

week

A **week** is seven days. There are 52 **weeks** in a year.

weigh

(weighs, weighed, weighing)
You put something on a scale and **weigh** it to see how heavy it is. *The potatoes **weighed** ten pounds.*

weird

(weirder, weirdest)
If something is **weird,** it looks or acts strange. *The monster looks **weird** with two heads.*

welcome

(welcomes, welcomed, welcoming)
When you **welcome** people, you give them a pleasant greeting. *The girl* **welcomes** *her friend to the party.*

well

(better, best)
1. If you do something **well,** you do it in a good way. *The man and woman danced very* **well** *together.* 2. If you are feeling **well,** you are healthy and not sick.

were

(be, am, are, is, was, been, being)
Were is used to show that something occurred. *The children* **were** *running down the hill to the park.*

west

West is a direction. The sun sets in the **west** in the evening.

wet

(wetter, wettest)
When something is **wet,** it is full of water, like a **wet** sponge, or covered with water, like a **wet** road. *The friends got* **wet** *when they went swimming.*

whale

A **whale** is a huge ocean animal that looks like a fish but is really a mammal. *A blue* **whale** *breathes through a spout in its head and is the largest animal in the world.*

what

When you use **what,** you ask about the identity or makeup of something. *Do you know* **what** *questions the teacher will ask on the quiz?*

wheat

Farmers grow **wheat,** a type of grain on tall stalks. We grind the **wheat** seeds to make flour for bread.

wheel

A **wheel** is shaped like a circle and rolls around. A **wheel** moves things along the ground, like cars, bicycles, and skateboards.

wheelchair

A **wheelchair** is a type of seat with large wheels. You use a **wheelchair** when you are sick or cannot walk.

when

You use **when** to ask or tell about a particular time. *Do you know **when** the movie begins?*

where

You use **where** when you want to know about a place. ***Where** should I hang my coat?*

whether

You use **whether** when you want to know if it is or was true that something happened. *Do you know **whether** or not the train left on time?*

which

You use **which** when you want to know about a specific person or thing. ***Which** piece of fruit will the boy choose, the apple or the banana?*

while

While means at the same time as something else is happening. *The girl played a game on the computer **while** her friend read a book.*

whiskers

Whiskers are long, stiff hairs that grow on a man's face, like a beard. **Whiskers** also grow on either side of the nose on the faces of some animals, such as a cat.

whisper

(whispers, whispered, whispering) When people **whisper,** they speak in a very quiet, low voice. *The girl **whispers** a secret in her friend's ear, so no one else can hear it.*

whistle

A **whistle** is a small instrument that, when someone blows into it, makes a sharp, high-pitched sound. Police officers blow **whistles** to move traffic along.

white

When something has no color, it is **white.** Snow is **white.**

who

When you use **who,** you are asking about the identity of a particular person or group. ***Who** do you think ate all of the Halloween candy?*

whole

If something is **whole,** it has all of its parts and is not broken. *The last cookie on the plate is **whole.***

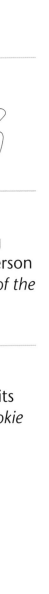

why

Why means for what reason, cause, or purpose. *The boy asks his teacher **why** the duck has webbed feet.*

wide

The distance from one side of something to the other is how **wide** it is. *A car is too **wide** to go on that patch.*

wife

(wives)
A man's **wife** is the woman he married.

will

Will refers to something that is going to happen in the future. *Debbie **will** carry the groceries for her grandmother.*

win

(wins, won, winning)
When you come in first in a race or a game or do better than other players, you **win**. *The boy **won** first prize in the chess match.*

wind

Wind is fast-moving air. *The **wind** blows the leaves down the street.*

window

A **window** is an opening in a hall or car that lets in sunlight and air. Most **windows** are covered in glass.

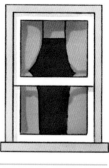

wing

A **wing** is a part of a bird's body that helps it to fly. Birds, bats, and insects flap their **wings** to fly. A metal airplane **wing** does not flap.

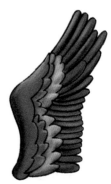

winter

Winter is the season that comes between fall and spring. **Winter** is the coldest season of the year.

wipe

(wipes, wiped, wiping)
If you **wipe** something, you clean or dry it by rubbing it with a cloth. *The boy **wiped** the dishes with a towel.*

wise

(wiser, wisest)
If someone is very **wise,** she is aware of what is going on, and she has good sense. *The **wise** girl brought along an umbrella in case of rain.*

wish

(wishes, wished, wishing)
If you **wish** for something, you want it or hope very much that it will happen. *The boy **wishes** for a puppy for his birthday.*

witch

(witches)
A **witch** is a person thought to have magic power. In stories, **witches** might ride on brooms or cast spells.

with

1. If you are doing something **with** someone, you are doing it together. *The boy is playing **with** his friend.* 2. You may use **with** to show that someone is using something. *The lady is writing **with** a pen.*

without

Without means something is missing. *The girl had to play the piano **without** her sheet music.*

wolf

(wolves)
A **wolf** is a wild animal that looks like a dog with a pointed nose, pointed ears, and sharp teeth.

woman

(women)
A **woman** is a grown-up girl.

wonderful

If something is **wonderful,** it is excellent. *My new haircut is **wonderful.***

wood

Wood is the hard part of the tree that comes from the trunk and branches. You can build houses and furniture with **wood.**

woodpecker

A **woodpecker** is a bird that taps holes in trees with its long, sharp beak. A **woodpecker** finds insects to eat in the small holes and makes a nest in the large trees.

word

A **word** is a group of sounds and letters that means something when put together. When you speak or write, you use **words.**

A B C D E F G H I J K L M N O P Q R S T U V W X Y Z

work

(works, worked, working)
1. **Work** is when you do a job or something that needs to be done. *My mommy **works** as a doctor.* 2. When something **works,** it runs smoothly and does what it is supposed to do. *My flashlight **works** with the new batteries.*

world

The **world** is the planet we live on, with all of the people and the things in it.

worm

A **worm** is a long, thin animal without arms and legs that lives in dirt. **Worms** are soft and small.

worry

(worries, worried, worrying)
If you **worry,** you feel anxious that something bad might happen. *I **worry** that my scary nightmares will come true.*

worse

(bad, worst)
If something is getting **worse,** it means it is already bad and getting very bad. *My hurt finger is much **worse** today.*

would

Would means to have a wish or desire to do something. *I **would** like to have fifty cents to buy ice cream.*

wreath

A **wreath** is a pretty wall hanging. **Wreaths** are often made from small branches or straw. You decorate a **wreath** with flowers, ribbons, and ornaments.

write

(writes, wrote, written, writing)
To **write** is to mark letters and numbers with a pen or pencil on a surface. People most often write on paper.

writer

A **writer** is a person who puts her thoughts down on paper or at the computer and writes for a job. A **writer** writes books and articles for magazines and newspapers.

wrong

Wrong means something is not right. *We took the **wrong** turn in the road, and now we are lost.*

X ray

An **X ray** is a photograph of your insides. You can see your bones on an **X ray.**

xylophone

A **xylophone** is a musical instrument with rows of wooden or metal bars. You play a **xylophone** by hitting the bars with small hammers.

yard

1. A **yard** is a measurement. There are three feet in one **yard** on a yardstick.
2. A **yard** is an open area next to a building with flowers or bushes. *The children like to play in the **yard.***

yawn

(yawns, yawned, yawning)
When you **yawn,** you open your mouth wide and breathe in and out because you are tired. Sometimes people stretch their arms out when they **yawn.**

year

A **year** is a measure of time. There are twelve months in one **year.**

yell

(yells, yelled, yelling)
When you **yell,** you open your mouth and shout loudly.

yellow

Yellow is a bright, sunny color. Lemons, bananas, and egg yolks are **yellow** foods.

yes

You use **yes** to show you agree. ***Yes,** I will help you clean up the yard.*

yet

Yet means up to this time. *The baby cannot feed herself **yet.***

A B C D E F G H I J K L M N O P Q R S T U V W X Y Z

A B C D E F G H I J K L M N O P Q R S T U V W X Y Z

you

You means the person being addressed. *You must meet me at the store.*

young

(younger, youngest)
A person or an animal that is **young** has lived only for a short time. *A colt is a young horse that still needs its mother.*

your

Your means that it relates or belongs to you. *This is your big brass tuba.*

yo-yo

A **yo-yo** is a round toy that looks like a flat spool on a string. The string winds around the **yo-yo** so you can make it go up and down and spin.

zebra

A **zebra** is an African animal that looks like a striped horse.

zero

Zero is another name for nothing. A **zero** is a math symbol that means none.

zip

(zips, zipped, zipping)
If you **zip** something, you open and close it with a zipper. *Zip up your sweater so you will stay warm.*

zipper

A **zipper** is a clothes fastener with two rows of metal or plastic teeth. You can have a **zipper** on your jeans or jacket.

zoo

A **zoo** is a place where wild animals, such as tigers and elephants, are kept so that people can come and see them.

zucchini

(zucchini)
Zucchini is a squash that is dark green on the outside and white on the inside. **Zucchini** grows on vines.

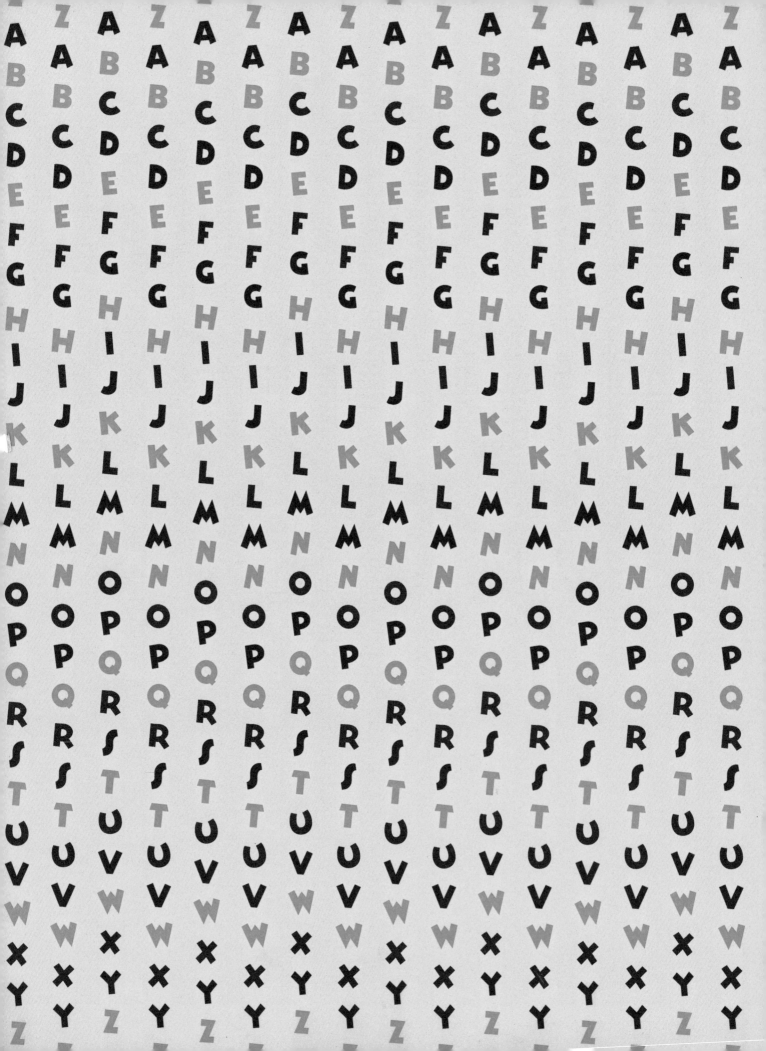